The PALACE and the PUNKS

Also by Tony Hill
If The Kids Are United

'For younger fans, there is an intoxicating account of the run-in to Fergie's first title triumph in 1993, while older fans will relish exhilarating memories of United in the 70's, a decade of Cup finals and cock-ups. Equally entertaining is Hill's witty and often poignant portrayal of a youth spent in a declining mining community...Impassioned and bleak but also hilarious.'
Manchester UNITED magazine

'A witty insight into the loneliness of the long-distance red. Like Hill's life, the book is balanced between two worlds – the very real world of Jacksdale, and the almost mythical world of Old Trafford, which haunts the young Hill's mind much in the same way as Atlantis must have menaced the infant Captain Nemo. And while it's hard to describe villages like Jacksdale without straying into parody, Hill describes his village and his family with wit and pathos.'   ★ ★ ★ ★ ★ *Four Four Two*

'A veritable collection of football stories from Hillsborough to Busby, Scargill to flares. It's a refreshing perspective from a non-Manc Red and it has poignant recollections from 70's Cup finals and 80's hoolie days.'   *United We Stand*

'This story of a Red growing up in a pit village during the 70's and 80's is both funny and sad at times...A great read.'
4/5 Glory Glory Man United

'A laddish feast of music, football and autobiography. Hill's passion for the game shines out like floodlights at a night-time match.'   *Nottingham Evening Post*

'Hill can be funny, but really finds his voice in harrowing recollections of the Hillsborough tragedy.'   *Daily Mail*

'Tony Hill made his momentous decision to become a Red Devils supporter in the 1970's and for the next twenty-two years lived and breathed to bag a Cup Final ticket. In this hilarious debut, Hill describes his consistently thwarted attempts to get his hands on the elusive voucher.' *EGO*

'A days-of-our-lives view of Man United from the wilderness years of the 70's to the rattling rise of Fergie's Red army.'

★★★★ *Total Football*

'A very funny look at every day life in the East Midlands.'

Mansfield Chad

'One of the best football books of the decade.'

When Saturday Comes

www.manutdbooks.com

The PALACE and the PUNKS

Tony Hill

NORTHERN LIGHTS LIT

Nowhere Man Please Listen

So President John F. Kennedy stayed at a farm in Jacksdale? Allegedly this was just five months before his assassination in June 1963 when he was visiting the grave of his sister Kathleen at Chatsworth House in Derbyshire.

I found this priceless nugget of mythical information on internet encyclopaedia site Wikipedia one rainy day.

It's typical of the humour of the village that when I raise this rumour in a local pub an old guy sat in the corner, nursing the last dregs of his pint of mild, taps me on the shoulder with his walking stick.

'Ah that's raight, Kennedy came in here fer a game o dominoes and pint o best, had a secret meeting wi Lee Harvey Oswald...'

Laughter echoes around the bar...

'Then t'other week after Muhammad Ali popped in wi Beatles. Soft than grease bollocks.'

More laughter.

'Yeah but Billy Fury did come in here for a pint of best and several other pop stars in the Topper days,' puts in a guy stood at bar.

'Ah nah that is true.'

Yes it is.

So maybe JFK assassination conspiracy theorists don't have to pack their bags and head on down to Jacksdale. Doubt they'd find it anyway. Pre the Internet and Sat Nav age it didn't appear on any maps. Even now if you order something - that has to be delivered - time after time they turn up about five hours late with the same excuse from the driver –

'Sorry mate, never heard of Jacksdale, it's not on the map and the Sat Nav system sent me to a dale, but it weren't Jack's.'

See? That fits in, the ideal out of the way place for the CIA to place JFK, then pick him up in the helicopter from a glade and whisk him away for the short flight to Chatsworth?

May be the Kennedy rumour was spread on the net by some local desperate to get Jacksdale on the map. It's a vast improvement on all the village was known for on the Internet about ten years ago. Back then if you typed 'Jacksdale' and 'history' into the search engines you'd achieve a 'Google whack,' that's just one return. And that was on the 'Nowhere Guide.'

Some smart arse had put something like 'All there is in Jacksdale is a rickety old skateboard ramp at the back of Woody's Club and loads of people like my gran, who plays bingo all the time and complains about my music and appearance.' Well yeah I know the feeling, but, you lazy git, if you dig a little you'll find there's a whole spaghetti junction of roads leading to everywhere.

On the wooded hills above the village stood Codnor castle. In 1415 local men gathered there, picked up their longbows and rode off to fight in the Battle of Agincourt. Tony Robinson's Channel 4 *Time Team* did a dig there and found the single most valuable item they've ever found on the show, a Henry V gold noble coin (1413 – 1422).

A major artery of the industrial revolution, the Cromford Canal (the site of the world's first factory), gave birth to the village. The pit and the miners who worked there helped feed Britain's growing economic monster.

Famous writer D. H. Lawrence came dancing in Jacksdale. The only German prison of war to escape from England during

World War 2 (as featured in the film *The One That Got Away*) did so from a POW camp a few miles away, made his way across country, down through woods, found himself in Jacksdale, nicked a residents bike and caught a train at the local station. It was my mate Jeff Fenn's (aka Feff, later to appear in this story) grandad who sold him a ticket.

World Motor Cycle GP champion Barry's Sheen's team-mate John Newbold was from the village.

I could say our MP was cabinet minister and defence secretary - at the time of the Iraq war - Geoff Hoon, but I doubt he knows where Jacksdale is, I've certainly never seen him down here, for all he knows weapons of mass destruction could be buried here.

So what have we got so far? Connections to one of the most famous battles in England's history, the birth of the industrial revolution, one of the greatest writers in English literature, a famous World War 2 story.

I sometimes think a series of lay lines converge under the village. Eat your heart out residents of the more well-known settlements in the district i.e. Mansfield, Sutton-In-Ashfield and Kirby-in-same-place.

What's their claim to fame; Sutton-In-Ashfield? Oh it has the biggest sundial in Europe, (perhaps that's because the local miners had plenty of time on their hands after Thatcher closed nearly all the Nottinghamshire pits?). It came third in the *Sunday Times* list of the most English towns in the country. That doesn't mean it's full of Morris Dancers, cricket on the green, medieval jousting (although a kind of version of that takes place in the local pubs and clubs on weekend nights) and loads of quaint little café's serving tea and cream scones. No it's so English because ethnic minorities are barely that. And Giles Brandreth is descended from there.

Kirkby? Not bad, Harold Larwood, the bowler who tried to decapitate the Ausies in the famous Ashes test match series of the 1930's is from there.

Mansfield? Daniel Defoe passed through on his tour of Britain in 1725 and commented 'I came to Mansfield, a market town but without remarkables.' Coo-a-choo Alvin Stardust came from there, it was voted 6th worst place to live in a Channel 4 poll, and this guy was buried alive in a coffin in a pub garden to set a record for doing so, even though it's not recognised by the *Guinness Book of Records* (apparently his mum did it first in the 1960's).

So there you go, not a patch on Jacksdale's history, if the residents of those towns protest and have more to say, then write your own bloody story. And I'm not even finished with village's claim to fame yet.

Marc Almond of Soft Cell fame had his school re-union in the Royal Oak. This is mainly because his best mate (and one of my friends now) from his school days, Chris Haliday, lives down here. He was the first person the young Almond had a crush on (it's true, go to the index section of his autobiography and look up Hailday, Chris) although I'd better point out that Chris is heterosexual, lives with long term partner Trina and has a couple of children, so Almond's love was unrequited.

Then we come to Fred Dibnah, yes *the* Fred Dibnah, steeplejack extraordinaire and esteemed industrial historian, who stopped off to take photos of Jacksdale on his farewell tour.

Actually that's not what I was coming to, but it's noteworthy all the same. No, now it's time to mention the music venue the Grey Topper, the subject of this story. Not heard of it? Well if you're not from this area you didn't know about all of the above did you? A surprising number of people have heard of the Grey Topper and an even more surprising line up of groups and singers appeared there between the late 1960's and early 80's.

I mean what other village in England could have for their local entertainment (as an alternative to a game of bingo at the Miners Welfare) – Bill Haley and the Comets, Billy Fury, Ben E King, The Sweet, The Stranglers, Simple Minds, Adam and the Ants, The Specials, Pretenders, The Ruts, Toyah, Ultravox, to name but a few. Ok, ok so half appeared there after their star had lost its shine and the New Wave groups came here before they made it big.

I love music though, it's my main drug and I've been to loads of gigs over the years. What I've always prided myself on is getting into groups early before they've had chart success and the masses latch on and inevitably they sell out. That's often when groups are at their best live, the early days, as I'm sure the surviving members of The Beatles, Sex Pistols (who incidentally were in negotiations to play the Grey Topper) and Nirvana would admit.

So those lucky village residents who's local was the Grey Topper, Jacksdale, between 1969 and 1981 were fortunate indeed, even if at the time they didn't realise it. Like leaving early, to get a fish supper and mushy peas in from the chippy, whilst a John Foxx lead Ultravox is pioneering electronic music. Having their back to the stage, propping up the bar and chatting up a local girl, talking about the days shift down the pit or the fortunes of the local football teams as The Stranglers and Vibrators are heralding in the punk explosion.

By 1979, though, the word had spread far and wide that the Grey Topper was the place to be for the punk and New Wave scene. This was the year of the final rise and fall of the now infamous venue.

BABYLON'S BURNING 8

Winter 1979

'How's your hands during this cold and frosty weather? Here is a good hand cream recipe. It makes up into a good half pound. 4oz. Lanolin, 4oz petroleum jelly, 1oz almond or olive oil and 1oz rose water.

Warm the lanolin…..'

It's the coldest winter for 15 years, blizzards sweep in from the Steppes of Siberia testing the resolve of a local hermit – and his best friends, which are two dogs and five cats - who's slept out under the stars since the 1920's depression. 'I wanted to be a cowboy but my parents wouldn't let me sail to America, so I became one here.' His gun slinging days are now over, he's old and retired from shooting squirrels for the pot. Generous locals are bringing him soup.

For a joiner, though, the heavy snow proves a blessing, he's making a killing making and selling sleds. Not that we could afford them on our council estate, we had to improvise before we excitedly rushed to our own version of the Cresta Run, hewn out of the snow drifts blocking Palmerston Street.

Coal sacks, plaggy bags and old washing machine tin lids were our toboggans. Those of us who'd used the latter would have to face the wrath of angry mums all over the estate, who went to the wash place (a shed attached to the house) to clean their husbands dirty pit clothes and find they can't until the machine lids were in place, sleeves were rolled up and rolling pins were at the ready for our return.

I guess if I'd saved up my pocket money I could have bought a sled and saved myself a bollocking. But I'd much more important things to spend it on, a skateboard for a start, the one I had was one my dad had knocked together, by cutting up a piece of plywood into a rectangular shape (he could have at least sanded some curves on there), then dismantling a pair of my sisters old roller skates for the wheels. I felt totally uncool turning up to the Westdale enders skate park (even if that was also DIY, being just an old door on milk crates) even though I'd tried my best to make it look so, painting on an anarchy symbol and plastering it with motorbike stickers I'd nicked from my brothers *Motorcycle News*.

Other cash went on anything, and I mean anything football, especially my team Manchester United, even though it was now uncool to support them as local team Forest were champions and had just knocked Liverpool out of the European Cup.

I also had a new passion eating up most of my pocket money, pop music. I'd started my record collection the previous autumn after seeing Public Image Ltd, The Boomtown Rats and Elvis Costello on *Top of the Pops*.

My sister, brother and me used to play a cruel trick on mam. Every Saturday when she went out shopping we'd give her a list of the singles we wanted her to get for us. She'd laugh at the names of the groups and song titles.

'Banana Splits' by The Dickies (who's name on the cover was in the shape of a dick), Ian Dury and the Blockheads, 'Hit me with your rhythm Stick' –

'You're winding me up, aren't you? They're not real groups.'

So from then on we would make up groups and songs and add them to the list for mam to ask for in the record shop. Then wait for her coming home Saturday teatime.

'Mam, did you get those singles we asked for?'

'Not all of them. I got the ones by Blondie, The Police and the Jam, but they'd never heard of "I Got An Itch" by The Spitting Shysters, or "Oi Pig, Up Yours" by Punky and Perky on pink vinyl.'

So for most of the time – apart from the raucous music coming out of teenagers bedroom windows – Jacksdale was pretty sedate, an ordinary northern working class village. There's nothing to cause concern in the news columns of the local papers –

A handful of people had become unemployed and there was the imminent closure of Teversal colliery. The coal board urged miners not to worry as 'there are plenty of jobs at other numerous pits in the area.' Many of which were regularly breaking output records. They had however called their offer for a three and a half percent pay increase 'a joke.'

The only things the village was in the news for was 1. The story of the Gate Inn landlord –

'Bob Moore proved regulars wrong when they warned him that a Bull Terrier and goat wouldn't mix, and is proving the point by taking the unlikely pair a walk around the village every morning. Along with resident cat Whiskey.'

'The locals expect scuffles on the pavement but the three are firm friends,' said Bob.

'I've caught the goat trying to sneak into the kitchen to steal vegetables.' Added wife Val.

2. The melting snow causing the perennial flood problems in the village, much to the annoyance of a local councillor.

Between The Devil And The Deep Blue Sea

Jacksdale residents have chance to choose their fate. They can either be knocked down by a car or be drowned, according to councillor Barry Smith after repeated complaints of 'ponding' – pedestrians being splashed by cars on Laverick Road. On numerous occasions they have had to dash into shop doorways to avoid a shower.

'One of these days there's going to be a nasty accident,' he warned. 'A pedestrian is going to get drowned or run over, depending which is the best way out.'

At the weekend, though, a new kind of flood was about to sweep into the village, a cultural one. Something was stirring at the Grey Topper. For the last year or so a small but ever growing bunch of teenage punk rockers - after Saturday trips down to the Kings Road in London – were taking over the northern soul nights. Demanding the DJ play the likes of The Clash, The Dammed, Siouxsie and the Banshees, and of course the Sex Pistols and showing disquiet at the 'has been groups' on stage.

Mick Clark: This might sound arrogant but there would have been no punk scene in Jacksdale if it hadn't been for myself, Marsy and Spike. It was us who pestered the DJ to play punk records, and eventually he did. A gradual process starting with about two a night until we ended up with our own punk nights.

Nige Cockayne aka Spike: There was only a handful of us to start with. We'd go up to the DJ and tell him we were sick of disco and soul, he'd reluctantly put some punks records on and we'd throw ourselves about the dance floor. All these soul boys, many from Nottingham, stood around watching us, arms folded, scowling. 'Well these punk boys really know how to dance,' said the DJ sarcastically.

Jackie Simpson: He was a real medallion man and had one of those 3-wheel orange bug cars. It was only tiny with two seats, one day about six of us packed in to it for a trip to Skeggy, it only reached the bottom of the road before tipping over.

Spike: We didn't give a fuck, we were like 16 and knew our time was here. We were just kids when we got into punk. We were wandering the streets on a cold night with nowt to do, so we walked into this chapel. The preacher points us out and says 'This is what our society is becoming, it's the devils work, we must drive out the demons.' There were all these old dears that looked like they wanted to kill us. I thought this is alright, if punk gets this reaction.

Mick Clark: I remember quite clearly that all the so called 'grown up' lads had hair down to their fuckin arse, wore Wrangler denims and listened to Led Zeppelin and Queen, and to make it worse they all stunk of Brut 33 - wankers! I just didn't

13

get what the fuss was about, particularly with Queen, what a fuckin waste of time they were. I bought the Sex Pistols 'God Save the Queen' because I couldn't hear it anywhere, it blew me away, what a fantastic record, what an amazing band.

I was sent home from school because I had two safety pins on my blazer and a badge as big as a dustbin lid that read 'Mummy what's a Sex Pistol?' My parents were never comfortable with me listening to Bolan and Bowie, so punk was a big no no. I had to hide my records under my bedroom carpet. Happy days.

Soon a gang of them that included Spike, Marsy, Tink, Mick Clark and Feff were meeting up on Saturdays to get the train down to London and the fashionable punk hotspots - Beufort Market, Portobello Road and of course the King's Road.

Spike: The first time we went in Seditionaries, Vivienne Westwood and Jordan - both with huge blonde hair sticking up – were watching *Tiswas* and totally ignored us until it was done. Another time Mick was interested in this bright yellow mohair, this assistant pulled it over his head and tugged it down, ripping holes in several places in the process. 'Don't worry it looks better now, may even have to charge you more for it,' she said. I bought a red chaos armband and bondage trousers. It was expensive though £40 for some clothes.

Mick Clark: On my first visit to London I bought some black crushers from Robot, a mohair and a 'She's dead I'm Alive, I'm yours' t-shirt from Seditionaries. Jordan was in there and I was mesmerised, she was done up like the bride of Frankenstein, face all white, red contact lenses and purple hair pointing straight up, she was stunning, and the breasts, oh man! (I was only seventeen as the song goes).

Anyway, Jordan got chatting and asked us where we came from etc, then winked and put me a red chaos armband into my

14

bag and whispered 'our secret' and never charged me.

The original Jordan

Feff: They always took the piss out of our accents.

Spike: Then when you'd step out of the shop there'd be police searching you, looking for any excuse to arrest us. We were as naive as fuck. We went to this bar in Soho, £3 for a pint but you got two women or a knife in the back if you didn't pay. We were like no thanks we'll come back when we've saved up a month's wages.

Mick Clark: When we first started going out in our new gear the reaction from the locals ranged from hostile to ridicule. I clearly remember one of Marsy's old school mates refusing to speak to him while he wore 'those stupid clothes.' Never saw the twat again and I've long since forgotten who he was, but I bet the sad bastard is still in denims and listening to Deep Purple, the cunt looked like Danny fuckin Baker! - No loss, move on!

For every ten people that abused us and took the piss, one would come and ask us if they could come to London with us, and so it grew, and at an alarming rate.

Marsy: The Teddy Boys didn't like us. One night one grabbed me by the scruff of the neck and marched me to the edge of the village, 'Get out punk,' he yelled.

Mick Clark: Our crew was quite standoffish, if you weren't dressed right, we didn't talk to you. Sad I know.

They'd had a few New Wave and punk bands on before. The Stranglers appeared at the Grey Topper very early in their career (March 1976). Punk was in its infancy then and The Stranglers at that time had not been labelled as being punks. Their music was described as pub rock. In spring 1977 punk originals The Vibrators showed up. These groups were rare though, now the young crowd wanted more of the same. More of the New Wave. In March they started to get their wish. First The Pretenders, then The Members came to the Topper.

Mick Clark: We pestered Alf, the owner, to book punk bands and eventually he gave in and booked The Members. They were riding high in the charts at the time with 'Sound of the Suburbs' and when they played the Topper it was a huge night for Jacksdale and the Topper punks. Things would never be the same again.

Leaning On A Lamppost

With the newly discovered JFK Jacksdale association on my mind, I'm in luck as I call in at my parents at the other end of the village. Local historian, aka Tom the Plumber (who made the video 'Little Fanny Fletcher' about Jacksdale's history) just happens to be there fixing a bath panel.

'What's this about President Kennedy staying at a farm in Jacksdale Tom?'

'JFK! What stayed here?'

'Yes, when he went to visit his sisters grave at Chatsworth in 1963 apparently.'

'Not heard that one.'

'Oh.'

I'm disappointed he's not got more to tell me, perhaps he has but it's still classified and doesn't want to be taken out by the CIA whilst he's stopping a leaky tap. Still it's always fascinating to chat to him about local history and I've another subject on that to bring up with him.

On my way there I'd driven past the old picture palace/Grey Topper building and was dismayed to see it cordoned off and covered in demolition signs. We'd already lost one well-known drinking establishment The Portland Arms (where I spent many a happy hour, wish I could remember them mind) now the famous Grey Topper was finally to bite the dust.

I was hoping Griff Rhys Jones and the film crew of BBC 2's *Restoration* team would turn up in the nick of time with conservation experts Ptomely Dean and Marianne Suhr.

'Ohh look Marianne! A genuine working class fleapit. You can just picture the scruffy oiks crawling out of their holes in the ground, spitting on flannels to clean their faces and pinning together their Sunday best to spend a whole lot of their pittance of wages to watch wags like George Formby.'

'Yes Ptolemy and look! Look! What's this, punk lettering on the walls and hardened spit and snot. See? That got into the brickwork and eroded the mortar letting in the damp, and this floor, what a state it's in, all that pogoing has taken its toll.'

But they never did.

I'd thought about writing the history of the place after the publication of my first book, but with owner Alf Hyslop dying I assumed all the major stories had gone with him.

However, listening to Tom tell me about the picture palace days, and that his dad had memories of it, and the fact that the projectionist for 40 years Bill Parr, now 90, is still around, combined with seeing the demolition posters fires my imagination. Unless their dad or grandad has mentioned it, no one under the age of 30 knows about the legend on their doorstep. Time to put that right...

So let's go back to 1912. The year 'Memphis Blues' became a hit, the first of its kind to do so. Folk singer Woody Guthrie and blues man Lightnin' Hopkins were born. All of which were a significant influence on the rock bands playing the Grey Topper over 50 years later.

It's April - Henry Bensley is thousands of miles from England and half way through his trek. It was four years now since he'd taken up the bet, of £21,000 from two aristocrats in a London club, that he couldn't walk around the world, pushing a pram without being identified, hence the iron mask from a suit of armour.

He may have been tempted to lift his visor to check out the English newspaper headlines, if he'd come across them - Scott of the Antarctic was missing. He probably thought better of it though, if he was identified he'd lose his bet and anyway surely the great explorer would show up.

However if the story about Scott hadn't tempted him to lift his visor the story shortly afterwards surely must. Out in the Atlantic the 'unsinkable' RMS Titanic had had a date with the night and an iceberg. As it slowly began to sink, its bow rising out of the water, the band played on.

Thousands of miles away, on the safe terra firma of the English Midlands, down the Erewash valley on the boarder with Nottinghamshire and Derbyshire, another band were in final rehearsals for their big day, performing at the opening of the new modern Picture Palace in the industrial mining village of Jacksdale, as reported in the local press –

'With 650 seats, some of the plush red variety, artistically decorated, radiators throwing off a regular supply of heat, a stage and a Pathe bioscope flashing on screen pictures of an educational and instructive nature. Saturday matinees for the children and plans for theatricals and concerts this new palace of entertainment is a welcome addition to the village for the hard working residents to relieve the monotony of the common round of daily toil.'

Jacksdale had quickly become a bustling village, almost a mini, model town, with industry, a canal, railway station, shops, several pubs, a dance hall and now the palace. In fact, like in the days of the Grey Topper in the future, it attracted people from other towns and villages in the area, including a struggling writer from the nearby town of Eastwood as he mentioned in a letter to his agent.

'My sister and I were at a bit of a dance last night at Jacksdale – mining village four miles out. It was most howling good fun. My sister found me kissing one of her friends goodbye – such a ripping little girl – and we were kissing like nuts – enter my sister – great shocks all round and much indignation. But life is awfully fast down here.'

His name was D. H. Lawrence and he was working on *Sons and Lovers* at the time. Soon, though, his feelings had changed about the place.

'Here, in this ugly hell, the men are most happy. They sing, they drink, they rejoice in the land.'

This was probably after he'd been knocked out for not supporting a local football team or liking the right kind of music, a fate that would befall many an outsider over the years.

2006…I knock on the door of an end terrace on York Avenue in Jacksdale. Bill Parr answers the door, tall, sprightly, with a thicker head of hair than mine, he looks years younger than 90. He shakes my hand eagerly as he welcomes me in. His son is also there, and my village credentials are quickly put to the test.

'Who's yuh dad?' asks Bill's son Eric.

'Brian Hill.'

'Brian! Was talking to him today up Brinsley with yuh mum and nephews.'

'Yeah my brother lives up there.'

'Jack was yuh uncle then, Sue and Sandra yuh cousins. I

always had a shine for yuh aunty Janet,' he comments, glint in his eye.

I've passed, we're all at ease and without any prompting, like an old projector come to life, Bill reels out his story. I sit back in a red plush seat and let it unfold, I've not the cheek to ask for popcorn, maybe in the intermission.

'Tom Key wer first projectionist, mi dad Fred got a job helping him, part time, his main job wer dahn pit. This ere manager mester Hall used to sing to some films and Sid Robinson played piano. There wer an orchestra too at times, wi a harmonium, violin, somebody on drums and this double bass, a bloody gret big thing that this poor chap had to carry along canal tow path from Pinxton (a village about 2 miles away).

Mi dad eventually became the projectionist and when ahh wer eleven I started helping him. Yuh had t'goo up this spiralling iron staircase t'get t'projector room. I'd help him rewind films, but wi had t'do all sorts, tend boilers and gas engines – that provided the electricity – put posters up and clean the place. Most important job I helped mi dad wi wer changing reels, yuh had to be quick, tha wer only one projector in them days yuh see, so we had t'stop film and suffer raight chuntering, whistles and cat calls from crowd,' Bill laughs, then drifts off, like he's changing his own reel.

After a minute or so sat in silence I'm just about to ask what films were on but before I do so the second instalment is on.

'An Excursion in Jura Mountains wer a film I remember, wanted t'goo there, Pathe news kept us informed, A Shunter's Daughter that wer a good un....'

I'm intrigued what that was about but Bill's in full flow.

'Rio Rita was the first talkie in t'nineteen thirties, I'd taken over as the projectionist bah then. Then war came along. They used a window of a shop across road t'advertise what films were on, these big posters were illuminated by a spotlight on top of the palace, course when air raids started they had to turn that off and black everything out. Soon ahh wer off to do mey duty,

21

served in RAF and got a job showing pictures to the troops, and got paid for it!'

'You went back to the palace though?' I ask.

'Oh ahh, I mean I were like mi dad, worked dahn pit and palace as well, loved it. The forties and fifties wer hey day Roy Rogers and Trigger in *Utah, Hop A Long Cassidy, Flash Gordon*, it wer packed out for Saturday afternoon matinees.'

'Tell him about the floods,' suggests Eric.

There's a slight scowl.

'Always bloody flooding Jacksdale in them days, and palace was in the lowest spot. Back breaking it was.'

'Back breaking?'

'Yeah, a show would end, doors oppun up, only t'find there'd been another dahn pour an a moat wer surrounding t'palace. We had t'carry these big old women back t'dry land.' Bill's shakes his head.

'Don't forget the toilets,' says Eric.

'Ahh bloody toilets, women's wer alright they wer upstairs, but men's were dahn in basement, they could be underwater at times.'

'You'd need a divers suit to get in there, so we just pissed on top of the water,' puts in Eric.

'Could cause a raight stink, things could float out, wi had to have this lad ready with a fishing net.'

It all came to an end for the Palace though?

'Ahh, it wer on decline by t'late fifties. It wer that bloody idiot box there,' he nods angrily to the television. 'I mean they tried all sorts o things to keep cinema alive 3D, cinema scope but it wer no good,' Bill's eyes dim like the credits have done.

Roy Rogers and Trigger rode off into the sunset at the Palace on February 27th 1960.

'Any characters you remember from Jacksdale's past?' I ask to brighten the mood.

'Ahh remember mester Lymb, aye owned snooker hall across from the palace and had his fingers in other pies too. He had a gammy leg so they called him Nobby Lymb, he used to hobble around village, wi great expectations, kids running after him mocking his limp.

He did outings t'coast in his charabanc, but it couldn't get up one of bloody steep hills out of Jacksdale, so you had t'get aht and push, more hard wok and it wer supposed to be a day off.'

Then Bill and his son tell me about a character called Bob, who used to make too much of a racket at the cricket matches, ringing a bell and coming out with the odd sarcastic comment and being a little too drunk and disorderly. Unfortunately, on one occasion, this was when they were playing the police team who always turned up in a Black Mariah. He ended up being taken away in it, and getting dumped a few miles up the road.

Shortly after going to see Bill this elderly couple ring me up. It's strange, they must have a speakerphone as they're both talking to me and each other from a distance, like they're sat side by side on the settee, holding hands as nostalgia washes over them. Going back to their young courting days.

'Yes we sat on the back row a few times.'

They tell me about 'tuppenny rushes' being the 'treat of the week' and the Saturday matinees.

'When I wer lad our whole family went down to see George Formby in a film called *It's In The Air*. My dad had this pipe, he lit it up just as the film started, I were sat behind and all his smoke drifted up and blocked the screen, I turned to my brother and said yes it is up in the air isn't it.'

The couple are chuckling away to themselves.

'We didn't go t'Grey Topper did we?'

'Oh no, not the Topper, too much trouble.'

'That would be the alcohol you know.'

'Yes and that music, devil music we called it.'

'I heard there's evil messages hidden it.'

Ah Judas Priest, they could be right there.

Same old boring Sunday morning old mans out washing the car,
Mums in the kitchen cooking Sunday dinner her best meal moaning
while it lasts,
Johnny's upstairs in his bedroom sitting in the dark,
Annoying the neighbours with his punk rock electric guitar,
This is the Sound of the Suburbs

'Sound of the Suburbs' - The Members

Spring 1979

'Tim and Di will be on stage at Skegby Miners Welfare on Wednesday. Good reports for this duo.'

Hey Roy things are happening at the Grey Topper. The Members are on, they reached No.12 in the national charts.

'Sunday at the Aquarius is guitar vocal duo, The Edendales, very professional, very popular. It could be just the spot for a run out.'

Ok, next month maybe.

Heavy snow returns in March, snowdrifts block Palmerston Street and other lanes, Jacksdale's again cut off. A determined or perhaps nervous coach driver, egged on by an already drunk and rowdy load of Notts Forest fans, smashes his way out, taking them to Wembley to see Brian Clough's team beat Southampton 3-2 in the League Cup final and continue to challenge Liverpool to be the kings of English football.

To our delight, the school heating breaks down again, we're sent home and are back tobogganing down our Cresta Run. Dad, staggering home from the pub, falls into a drift and loses his watch. A month later when the thaw came, he finds it and jumps for joy as it's still miraculously working. He writes to the manufactures, thinking they'll want to use his story for an ad and send him a brand new top of the range one. They don't reply at all and then he accidentally smashes the old one with a hammer.

In other news –

Henry Cooper appears at a local store and splashes it all over.

Jacksdale's motorcycling ace John Newbold has a promising start to the season at Donnington Park finishing with a third, twice. Then finishes 3rd behind Suzuki team mate Barry Sheen in the *World Of Sport* Superbike event.

More excitement for us football mad kids. The FA are looking to turn the empty mansion Annesley Hall into the England football team training headquarters. It's only a bike ride away, so we're dreaming of mixing it with the likes of Steve Coppell, Trevor Francis and of course Kevin Keegan, several misguided lads have bubble perms in preparation.

On an industrial estate in the nearby village of Pinxton, my brother Brian finishes his days work at a printers, then waits outside the gate of another factory for his friend Peter Thompson to also clock off so they can walk back home together. He's going to wind him up again about being under the thumb of his girlfriend Lorraine.

The Thompson's used to live on our estate, Peter and his brothers would call for my brother and me on the way to school. Then they moved to Selston, but just across road from our grandparents so we continued to play football in the street with them and Peter would let me sit on his motorbike.

This day, though, Peter doesn't show, so Brian walks home alone. We hear the news later that Peter and Lorraine have gone missing after going for a walk in woods near Matlock, Derbyshire. Police say there's no cause for alarm as it will probably be just another case of teenage runaways.

Topper punks Mick Clark and Marsy were back from London with tales of the Beaufort Market riot.

Mick Clark: Me and Marsy went down to see The Clash protest gig against the closure of the Beaufort Market, they turned up and the police wouldn't let them play. Hundreds of punks ran riot as a result, the police response was really heavy handed.

Marsy: It was total chaos, pitch battles everywhere.

Mick Clark: It was quite a big riot and made the Sunday papers, good fun at the time. I was really pissed off though, because as we got to Seditionaries we found them closed in sympathy with Beaufort Market, bastards I'd gone for another mohair!

Down at the Grey Topper, after the success of The Pretenders night, they decided to book more New Wave acts.

First up was Doll by Doll with an eclectic mix of folk, blues, celtic, psychedelia and punk, and a singer called Jackie Leven who was once described as the 'bastard child of Elvis and Bowie.' He's now an acclaimed Scottish folk singer.

Next came The Jerks. Five teenagers from Yorkshire who, having witnessed the 'Anarchy In The UK' tour in 1976, got together in an old garage and plugged in to create their own blend of attitude, noise and disturbance. The result was 'Get Your Woofing Dog Off Me' for a growing gang of Topper punks to pogo to.

Phil Gilbert (guitarist/co-songwriter) – The Jerks: I think we played the Topper more than once – I remember a big out of town venue, which was very much on the punk circuit. A bit like a well lit set from the *Blue Velvet* film. A neon palace in the darkness, maybe shades of *Phoenix Nights*.

By April 79 we were bulging out into New Wave. My main memories were being attacked on stage by a disabled man's crutches and puking up out of the transit (proper ex- Northern Gas orange transit van, driven by the ageing Speedy John) on the way back. I had to wipe it off the side of the van and bung him another 10 on top of the agreed 15.

The real coup for the Topper came on Sunday 22nd of April. Already booked before their punk anthem 'Sound of the Suburbs' stormed up the charts to No.12, London's The Members were at the height of their popularity. I'd bought it and pogoed around my bedroom, all my mates had.

With its memorable intro, driving punk guitars and sardonic lyrics about the frustration of living in suburban mundanity, 'Sound of the Suburbs' spoke to a new generation of disillusioned kids across the UK.

Nick Tesco – The Members: That whole period was surrounded by so much societal violence, with the tabloids whipping up hysteria about punks, so that 'honest law abiding people' felt justified in going out and beating the shit out of kids.

28

I remember when it all first kicked off, kids like JC and I were growing up in pig ignorant suburban wildernesses like Camberley where the average Joe left school at 16, got a well paid job in the local electronics industry and pissed their money up against a wall every Friday and Saturday night. They all looked like Rod Stewart with flares and beat seven shades of shit out of anyone who looked different, by colour or trouser style. Funnily enough, even though times are as violent, kids don't seem to attack each other anymore for wearing the wrong kind of trousers.

The village had never seen anything like it that night. The older residents thought a space ship had landed. Hundreds of multi coloured, spikey tops poured through streets Topper bound.

Feff: Jeff Dunn sprayed his hair silver and blue with car paint. It wouldn't come out, he had to shave his head after the gig, so he didn't get the sack at work. I used orange juice or oxtails soup or something, anything around that colour to help spike up my orange hair. I can remember it dripping down my face walking home in the rain.

Spike: It should have been fifty pence to get in that night, but when Alf looked out of the window and saw this queue stretching around the block, he put the admission up to a £1 and let in twice as many as would usually be allowed in there.

Mick Clark: I think they broke the all time attendance record at the venue and it was a fantastic night. Alf made money so he was happy.

Nick Tesco: The first time we arrived in Jacksdale it was weird as fuck. We'd driven through the countryside and then we arrived in this village that was almost a cartoonist's idea of a grim mining village. I spent a lot of time, off and on, in Yorkshire growing up and it seemed similar to some of the villages up there. Being smart arse London wankers we mooched around, called the place a toilet and wanted to go to the hotel, unfortunately that was miles away. The gig, though, was awesome, it completely blew us all away, I've never forgotten it. The audience were some of the best people I ever met, but it was a spitfest.

Spike: I can still picture the moment this spotlight highlighted the guitarist – the rest of the band were in darkness – as he did the intro to 'Sound of The Suburbs', we went crazy. I was stood on a table, I pogoed up and down and it collapsed under us.

And there was all this stuff dripping off the ceiling onto everyone. I reckon it was the nicotine seeping out because it was so hot in there.

J C Carroll – The Members: They were possibly the smallest but most enthusiastic audience we have ever played to, the energy was unbelievable, the kids went madder than anywhere else in England.

Stephen Fletcher: The Members were great, but I also enjoyed the support band, which was Pinpoint, the lead singer was called Arturo Bassick, who had just left The Lurkers.

A couple of other things stick in my mind. I reckon it was Pinpoint who had a small dog with them, which ran across the stage, once or twice, while they were playing. I also remember a ferocious looking bouncer on the door, who I'm fairly sure was holding a length of bike-chain around his neck.

Nick Tesco: The problem was the bouncers. They were ugly, vicious bastards. The place was rammed and the crowd had nowhere to go but onto the stage. Our roadies were holding people back and keeping some clear space but then some bouncers waded in with pool cues and one of our crew got banged about a bit which pissed us off no end. I too remember the sweat mixing with the crap on the ceiling and dripping on everyone. It stained everything, with that and the spit it took a lot of cleaning.

The first time we played there was the best. It was like Rourke's Drift in the dressing room trying to keep the hordes out and our stuff safe. It was pretty humbling too, as we got drinking with a bunch of local lads who were a real laugh but they were telling us about their job and how they got to the coalface in the mornings. It kind of put all our prissy shit into perspective. I also got one shoe stolen! Why they didn't just steal the pair I don't fucking know.

The second time we played we were on our way down I guess. My favourite memory was talking to this kid, who was very pleasant, and then he came out with 'You used to be good, but now you're wank'. I used that as a motto for ages. That said we had a couple of the best gigs we ever played there.

Octopus and Chips

So the Picture Palace closed in 1960. When then did Alf Hyslop take over the building and open the Grey Topper? What other well-known performers appeared there that I don't know about? Are there any tour posters with the Grey Topper on, surely there are photos somewhere showing the inside....

Then I remember, in my pre *NME* reading days, as a kid, *Smash Hits* was my favourite magazine...no I lie *Shoot* was my favourite.....then again there was those well thumbed, slightly sticky ones a lad brought to school and charged 10p a minute to look at.

Yes in *Smash Hits* in the early 80's, they'd asked some pop star to name their worst gigs and the Grey Topper was one of them! Can't recall who it was or which band, one thing I am sure of is that I still have that *Smash Hits*, up in the loft of my parent's house.

A few years back they decided to turn my old bedroom into a guest room and play zone for my two little nephews (huh I noticed dad just happened to install a hi-fi and place his jazz records and books in there as well) So they put all my old stuff – including my pile of *Smash Hits*, *Sounds* and *NME*'s in a box and stored them in the trusty old loft.

Of course none of the boxes are labelled stating what's inside them. The first one I open resembles the toy version of 'how many people we can squash into a telephone box' if it had gone badly wrong, taped up and forgotten. The box is crammed with my sister's sorrowful looking teddies and dolls, several of which are decapitated.

The second box contains mam's entire Catherine Cookson books collection. Then I come across my brothers and mine Dinky and Matchbox cars collection and I'm really tempted to take them on down to play with them, then realise my nephews are coming around later and I have the excuse to do just that. Wow can't wait to shoot down Christy's dinosaurs with my

UFO interceptor.

The next box isn't the one I'm looking for but it's a great re-discovery. My 7' single vinyl record collection! I pull out several that are of significance to this quest – The Ruts – 'Babylon's Burning,' The Members – 'Sound of the Suburbs,' UK Subs – 'Stranglehold,' The Specials – 'Gangsters,' Toyah – 'Thunder In The Mountains,' and The Pretenders – 'Kid.' All cherished records of mine as a mini punk and all performed at the Grey Topper and apart from The Pretenders I never knew - at the time - that they were just down the road in my village.

I do now, have for many years, many of my mates, who are a few years older than me, saw them all and never stop rubbing it in.

I aim the beam of the torch through a tear in the next box and see it contains what I'm looking for, a pile of *Smash Hits*. I quickly open it up, then, on clocking the enormous spider, nearly have a heart attack. It's only after whacking it with the torch that I realise it's plastic and put there as a joke, to scare the person who open's this box....by me as a 14 year old!

Now leafing through the pages of *Smash Hits* I'm in 80's music hell - Bucks Fizz, Kajagoogoo, Modern Romance, Wham! (Fuck off!). Until there it is. 'Ten gigs I never want to play again.' No.1 is the Grey Topper, Jacksdale for Ultravox's Chris Cross! So it was the electronic music pioneers.

At the time I assumed this was 1979 with Midge Ure – just recruited from the Rich Kids – on vocals. Now I know Ultravox appeared at the Grey Topper in March 1977 and the John Foxx 'Underpass' single I'd also come across in my old vinyl collection was another connection to the Topper. He was the lead singer of Ultravox at the time and their sound was more akin to Roxy Music and Bowie, than the new romantic synth soundscapes of the Midge Ure lead outfit that would go on to sell millions of records with Top 10 hits like 'Vienna' and 'Dancing With Tears In My Eyes.'

TEN GIGS I NEVER WANT TO PLAY AGAIN By Chris Cross (Ultravox) (no particular order)

1. **The Grey Topper, Jacksdale.**
"There were more people in the fish shop opposite than at the gig."
2. **Vikings, Goole and the Top Hat, Spennymoor.**

Back in 77 their sound seems lost somewhere between glam and punk, and they were experimenting with electonica. This apparently wasn't half as appealing as a fish supper from the chippy for the Topper crowd though.

*

As I drive by the old Picture Palace/Grey Topper building the demolition team are inside removing its guts.

I'm off up to a library in a nearby town with my quest. There's bound to be mention of the Grey Topper in the old local papers. As a kid I can remember it making the front page on several occasions, and perhaps they advertised what groups were on in the entertainment section?

Stood at the information desk I can see two library assistants chatting in the back office, there is one sat behind the desk in front of me but she's transfixed on a computer screen. She resembles dog-training megastar Barbara Woodhouse. I give a little cough and she looks up.

I tell her I'm a writer and that they have my book on their shelves and what I'm trying to do.

Blank response.

I ask about local history documents and old newspapers.

'That's Jacksdale this isn't.' She replies and looks back at her computer screen.

'Well yes, but newspapers printed here covered the whole region including Jacksdale.'

Raised eyebrows.

'I'll think you'll find that the Grey Topper often appeared on the front pages of the local press in the 1970's, if not for trouble then to report on famous names appearing there like Bill Haley and the Comets!'

'Haley's comet?'

'No, Bill Haley and his Comets, famous rock 'n' roll star?'

Blank look.

'What about Adam and the Ants?'

Blank.

'The Specials, they sang where did you get that blank expression on your face?'

Blank.

'Ben E King, Bay City Rollers...' I name another 10...'Simple Minds?'

'Who has?'

'No they were a huge group in the eighties, don't, don't you forget about me.'

Raised Eyebrows, 'hope I do,' she mutters.

'Barbara Woodhouse?'

'Ah! We've a fantastic book on her here, in fact I've a signed copy at home.'

'Oh,' I touch my head in an apologetic manner. 'Sorry my mistake she cancelled the Topper to play Wembley Arena in front of 500 men and their dogs.'

There's a far away, perturbed look in her eyes like she's

spotted two pigeons copulating on one of the town's rooftops in the distance.

Another lady comes to the desk. I try her assistance.

'Is it possible to look at the local papers I'm researching the Grey Topper, Jacksdale?'

'The Grey Topper! Had some nights there in my younger days,' she replies, blushing, indicating the memories she has are not ones to associate with a demure looking library assistant. 'Met my first husband there,' she continues with a scowl. 'What years you looking for?'

By now I've been told that the Grey Topper opened in 1969. So ask for that.

She disappears into the back and returns with two huge folders containing every local newspaper for 1969. Daunted I carry them over to a desk. Soon though I don't care I'm stuck in a library on the hottest day of the summer so far, for over four hours I'm totally enthralled. I'll return there and other libraries many times, to be transported back to the 1970's.

I find just how quickly the place was established as the most 'happening' music venue for miles around. With a mix of beat groups, folk and psychedelia, it almost has the feel of some cutting edge club situated down an alleyway in the centre of some cosmopolitan city, instead of being stuck out on the edge of the Nottinghamshire coalfields. Well, on the nights they didn't play bingo, have on a sexist, racist comedian or old time dancing.

Roy Booker's predecessor, the more knowledgeable and adventurous Johnnie Singleton, is soon gushing in praise of the club and obviously spending perhaps too much time down there. 'Join the Grey Topper set, I'll think you'll enjoy yourself.' He's plugging it virtually every week.

It's the psychedelic bands that intrigue me most, with apt names like Jade Lemon, Orange Bicycle, The Magic Lanterns, Mosaic Sunset and Octopus. Soon I'm lost in their kaleidoscopic histories and music. It turns out that records by several of them are now sort after and highly collectable.

There's also a few surprise connections too, a couple of members of Octopus would join New Zealand New Wavers Split Enz, the creative talent behind Orange Bicycle - Will Malone would become a producer and do the string arrangements of The Verve's 'Bitter Sweet Symphony.' Then there's Ozzy Osbourne in The Magic Lanterns, but I'll save all that stuff for the coffee table A-Z section of the book.

Inside the Grey Topper in the early 1970's. He may be playing to one man and his dog (out of shot propping up the bar) but soon afterwards he joined a platinum selling super group.

The Japanese on the internet seem fascinated by obscure late 1960's British pyschedelia in particular, which can leave things a bit lost in translation...'Recorded in 69-70 in spite, it did not inhale, release it was not done even – to CD it was converted to the rare corner of the certain maniac store – contents already medium state of the cloud. This underground fork album, after a long time large excitation! – Think as the Floyd mysterious wind shelf - 2 women these is the Chimeras – the upper body naked lesbian...'

Thus describes my favourite band discovery from Topper 69. The acid-folk, psychedelic band called Chimera. They were fronted by two beautiful young women, Francesca Garnett and Lisa Bankoff. I downloaded some of their music from an album recorded in 1969. It was produced by Pink Floyd's Nick Mason, featuring Fleetwood Mac's Bob Weston and Orange Bicycle's Will Malone, it's sort of out there man! The song 'Mary's Mystery', which has trippy music with crashing symbols and bells, starts with these lyrics (sung with hand over the ear folk vocals).

'Ma-r-r-r-ry's mystery in the garden of SOMEWHERE, sh-e-e-e wanders through the night, the neighbours whisper between cups of tea that her eyes look strangely bright.'

Before going off into a Jimi Hendrix style guitar solo. It's LSD central. The miners at the Topper were more used to Lucy in the Sky with Double Diamond ale.

May – June 1979

'Ladies if you wear slippers to do the housework, then you'll be interested to know that most home accidents are caused by wearing them – particularly if they've grown large and sloppy.

When you think of all the walking and hours of standing we women do in the home, it does make sense that old shoes and baggy slippers are not good enough. We like to make sure our husbands and children are properly shod – we'll have to apply the same thinking to ourselves.'

In the news -

Frank Haynes snatches Ashfield back from the Tories in the General Election but Margaret Thatcher is the new Prime Minister.

Record outputs recorded across Notts coalfields, but there's a strike at Silverhill over working conditions and payment.

Forest become European Champions. Later the trophy is on display at our school, I queue up for my chance to get my hands on the famous trophy.

One local news story had become a national one. The bodies of Peter Thompson and Lorraine Underwood had been discovered in shallow graves near Cromford in Derbyshire.

I see these headlines doing my paper round which is on a lane on the very edge of Jacksdale, from here I can see the Crescent on a hill at the beginning of Selston, about half mile away, my grandparent's house and across road the Thompson's, tears run down my face.

'You having a laugh, you will be when Conway and Daily take to the stage at Pleasley Hill Working Men's Club.'

I'm sure sides will be split, but let's do rock steady as well Roy.

'New Wave rules OK at the Grey Topper, Jacksdale, tomorrow when The Specials pay a visit. This former night club is getting to be quite the place for punk fans.'

That's the man! But this is the first and last time Roy Booker mentions the Grey Topper. He quickly moves on to what's on at Huthwaite Miners Welfare –

'Don't miss comedy instrumental group The Koback Family and at the Sutton Social Club are Dixie Chicken.'

I was fascinated by an addition to my brother's record collection, a picture disc of 'The Worker' single by Fischer-Z. It had a picture of a train around the edge that looked great when spinning on the turntable, as a Talking Heads sounding song came out of the speakers. That same weekend, down Wagstaff Lane in Jacksdale, the band pulled into the Topper car park for New Wave night.

On the same week were Dafne and the Tenderspots. No I'd not heard of them either. And I was a bit wary of what results I'd get typing that into a Google search box (as I was for The Vibrators). What I wasn't expecting was Depeche Mode and Alan Wilder to show up.

The former keyboard player – and songwriter - with the electronica super group was known as Alan Normal in 1979 and was one of Dafne's Tenderspots.

Alan Wilder: As a young man I had an unwavering conviction (with hindsight, a kind of arrogance) that to become a successful musician was the one and only thing I would ever achieve. Part of this tunnel vision resulted in me joining a band called Dafne And The Tenderspots. They were a restaurant type group playing a mixture of jazz, R&B (in the traditional sense) and blues etc. I was roped in on keyboards for a few quid in my pocket and a free cheese, ham and tomato pancake at the end of the night (I got so sick of those things). We were also starting to write our own songs and, quite cynically, jumped onto the New Wave bandwagon after the explosion that had been punk rock. I went under the name Alan Normal and we had all these terrible clothes made and wore skinny ties.

Having auditioned numerous drummers and bass players, the line up that became Dafne & The Tenderspots was completed with Nick Monas on drums (a highly precocious, technically brilliant player who had absolutely no sense of 'less is more') and Steven Hughes (ex Burlesque) on bass. It was an odd mix and the music we came up with was inevitably bizarre - a mixture of quirky, stylised, convoluted New Wave jerkiness (a la XTC) mixed with jazz-rock double bass drum fusion, all fronted by Dafne herself singing from a blues and soul background. Contrived? You bet. We were awful, but again, we had a deal and made a single, 'Disco Hell' - the one and only single that was ever released.

Finally, after an uphill struggle, a fracas broke out over the ownership of the PA system and that was that. I think Graham and Dafne (who were an item - never a good thing in a band) moved out to LA to help reduce the effect of Dafne's unfortunate arthritis. I met up with them briefly one time during a Depeche Mode tour when they showed up at a show out there - a rather awkward after show meeting where we exchanged a few pleasantries and that was the last I heard.

I do look back at those character-building times, along with my other struggles and various unsuccessful ventures, with great fondness and appreciation of the grounding those experiences supplied. I remember supporting The Damned at the Wolverhampton Lafayette club once (which was a challenge). In fact, that was the night I first heard 'Warm Leatherette' by The Normal, which left a very strong impression - sounded like it had just landed from outer space. The Tenderspots played some real dives, some ok shows, drove all night in cold vans, lived on next to nothing - all the usual clichés. It didn't seem romantic at the time but I guess it was. I cite this period as the main reason for my subsequent appreciation of what I have been lucky enough to achieve since.

By June Jacksdale had become a Tourists hot spot. No not hordes of Japanese following the D.H. Lawrence trail or a group of JFK conspiracy theorists from Wisconsin checking out the village's mysterious connections to their president. I'm talking about the band The Tourists who took to the stage on Saturday 16th June 1979, flush with their £125 fee (for the whole band) in their pockets, to perform 'It's so good to be back home again.'

Lead singer Annie Lennox probably wished she was back home again as she dodged globules of phlegm. 'I only want to be with you' she sang next with heartfelt emotion, looking across at lover and band mate Dave Stewart.

Both singles would be in the Top 10 later in the year, but their image – Lennox in second hand Oxfam clothes, peroxide blonde hair and heavy blue eye mascara looking like a bedraggled Bet Lynch behind the bar in *Coronation Street* – and annoyingly catchy jingly New Wave pop, was far removed from the reinvented, futurist, synth powered, slick looking Lennox and Stewart band The Eurythmics, who 4 years later were at No.2 in the charts (No.1 in America) with 'Sweet Dreams.'

*

2009…My sister Elaine can't believe it now when I phone her in Manchester and I tell her about this Grey Topper project and the groups that played there.

'Where was I when all this was going on?' (She was 19 in 1979).

Ironically she missed all the punk and New Wave acts and future world famous groups, as she was probably the first in the village to get into punk - she was showing me pictures of the new fashion in *Honey* and *19* magazines in 1976 – and under it's influence had left home to go to art college (later onto uni doing fashion design).

I remember how excited I was in 1977, aged only 11, when I put on my straight jeans she'd bought for me, and checked my cropped hair in the mirror, before she took me down to Slab Square in Nottingham to meet up with her punk boyfriend, there were loads milling around, they made a real fuss of me and called me 'baby punk.'

By June 1979, ahead of the game as usual, she'd moved on from the scene. Elaine was home from college for the summer and we went for a walk around the village.

'Punk's out,' she told me.

'What's in then?' I replied disappointed.

'Mod and ska music.'

45

'Mod, sounds a bit puffy, what do they wear?'

'Smart clothes, pork pie hats, fish tail parkers?'

'Fish tails, stupid or what, you'd look a right twat.'

'Not an actual fish tail,' she laughed.

We were passing the Topper, a group pulled into the car park. On the side of the van it said 'Breaker,' I'd never heard of them, and even Elaine hadn't and she knew all about music. Thinking they were not worth hanging about for we walked on.

Roddy Radiation - The Specials: It was a mate of Horace's van, blue a bit like a transit, they were in a soul band called 'Breaker' and their name was still on the van. We did The Clash tour in it. It was a bit cramped with us all packed in, we stole a big judo mat, and put it on the top of the gear and most of us lay on that. It didn't help that Jerry (Dammers) had very smelly feet.

So what did he think of Jacksdale when they turned up there?

Roddy Radiation: I grew up in a tough mining village myself, just outside of Coventry, so picked up on the vibe of the place. I still go back to my mum's most Sunday's, but the pits closed and it's changed a bit, but it can still be a bit rough at times. We played anywhere and everywhere at that time, mostly small clubs and pub type backroom venues for very little money usually.

With a fusion of punk and ska, dressed as mods, the groundbreaking Coventry outfit were at a pivotal time when they arrived at the Grey Topper. Their first single 'Gangster's' had been pressed and was just a few weeks from release on their own 2 Tone label. Radio 1 legend and hugely influential John Peel had just broadcast their first session, the tracks were - 'Gangsters', future No.1 single 'Too Much, Too Young,' 'Concrete Jungle' and 'Monkey Man.'

Roddy Radiation: That was a breakthrough for us doing the John Peel show. I met him at a festival in Belgium once after our show. Horace was listening to John's words of wisdom in his back stage caravan. I stumbled in slightly drunk and interrupted John, so Horace slapped my face! I didn't think I was that out of order? But Horace did love his heroes whereas me, being a punky type chap, didn't always show some stars the respect they deserved, like John Peel did.

I wrote 'Concrete Jungle' about violence on the streets where I lived in Coventry at the time, Hillfields, which had a certain reputation. My song 'Rat Race' was about rich spoilt students wasting their time before going to jobs their rich daddies had lined up for them...makes even more sense now you have to be wealthy to be able to afford a university education!

The Topper punks weren't really ready for this new sound and didn't appreciate being wound up by The Specials followers.

Tink: There were all these youths in pork pie hats and suits, taking the piss and saying punk's dead, we're in. I'm surprised it didn't kick off.

Roddy Radiation: Yeah we had a few Coventry kids who were a pain in the ass. It got even worse later. We never usually saw any trouble from punks, it was skinheads who caused the problems - mostly right wing, but sometimes it was just fighting over rival football teams, different towns etc.

A lot of early punks adopted the rude boy look as The Clash had, in fact I'm 100% sure Dammers got the idea from Paul Simonon when we supported The Clash. He would usually turn up at gigs dressed in tonic suit, pork pie hat, Fred Perry and Docs.

Punk was the thing at the time when we first formed

47

1977/78. Me and Terry both fronted local Coventry punk bands (The Wild Boys & The Squad). The Specials played a mismatch of reggae and punk - Jerry suggested fusing what we had with ska, apparently Brad (John Bradbury, the drummer) had loaned him a ska album when they shared a house together in the mid 70's, he also loaned him a Sun-Ra album at that time - Brad says he never got either back!

I was into Bob Marley at the same time as punk and also listened to the virgin front line stuff and my sister-in-law's Rasta boyfriend had loaned me some U-Roy and I-Roy albums.

Early pre-2 Tone suit Specials. Note Roddy's punk gear.

I ask Roddy if playing the likes of the Grey Topper in the early days, when they had such a strong desire to make it, is when the band was at its closest and they did some of their best gigs

Roddy Radiation: I was still working in the daytime as a painter and decorator, so it was a bit tough. But when you're young you don't seem to mind. But yeah, guess you're right? We were hungry, angry and honest? Before the drugs, drink, girls and bullshit music business ruined us. We weren't one of those bands who'd been friends at school, so there was no strong bond holding us together later on.

Back in the summer of 79 it was great though, a few weeks after playing the Grey Topper 'Gangster's' went Top 10 and we were on *Top Of The Pops*. Most of us got drunk the first time on that. Me and Brad were escorted out of the BBC after I'd had a go at one of the top guys there for pushing in front of me at the bar. Having to be there early morning until early evening and being told what to do made it seem like being back at school, so after a few drinks we acted accordingly.

The brilliant, inspirational Specials, were at the forefront of the ska and mod revival. After seven Top 10 hits they split shortly after their finest moment, 'Ghost Town' - a kick in the teeth to Thatcher's Britain - was probably the best protest song to reach No.1. At the time I first spoke to Roddy there had been reports in the music press of a reunion.*

Roddy Radiation: Jerry's the boss. And unless he thought we would completely obey him - musically and image wise - he wouldn't reform the band. And I think he's a hypocrite, paranoid dictator. But then I would wouldn't I?'

---

*In 2009 The Specials did reform, but, as Roddy said, without Jerry Dammers. I would be there to see them at Glastonbury and Roddy would put me on the guest list for their gig at Rock city.

Coal Village Confidential

I'm starting to get a feel for what it was like in the Topper in the early 1970's and this is enhanced a whole lot further when an appeal for information goes out in a free local newspaper that's distributed to Jacksdale and three neighbouring villages.

It's evident that by 1971 the Topper had already become the place to be for the youth of the area.

Gary Roe: I'd left school at 15 and had my first wage packet from the pit burning a hole in my pocket. My mate Pud Rice, who was still at school, asked if I fancied a ride to the Grey Topper at Jacksdale. I hadn't got a clue what the Grey Topper was or where Jacksdale was either. It sounded like a western cow town.

Friday night came around and I dolled myself up, topped off with a bit of my dad's Old Spice aftershave. Blues Sta's (Sta-Prest), a Ben Sherman shirt, but the giveaway the black Dr Marten's boots (trademark of a Skin). I walked it to Kirkby and met up with Pud and we caught the Midland General B7 bus to Jacksdale.

We walked into the foyer and up to a counter, where we were challenged by two these two older guys with Teddy Boy style haircuts.

'Are you members?' One asked.

We weren't expecting this. I stood back and looked at Pud.

'No, how much is it?' He asked

'Half a dollar,' came the reply, which used to be 2/6 or half-a-crown. Now it is 12 and a half new pence.

We paid up, we'd come this far so we may as well go the whole hog and forked out the coins. It showed them we were men of means, workers, pitmen. To our amazement they never challenged us, took our money and gave us membership cards.

Boy did we feel grown up. We headed for the darkened dance hall, noticing the stage and some music to our liking coming from the larger than life speakers. The brew was Younger's Tartan and not Home, Kimberly or Shipstones we knew. It was 12p a pint. The drink was ok and quenched a miner's thirst after a hard week down the pit, or even a steady week watching safety films like *Mine Fights Dust, Fire on 69's.*

Soon the place began to fill up with regulars and we tried to blend in. We watched in anticipation for Greebo's, if they showed up we were high tailing it down the road as fast as our Airwair boots would carry us. The punters looked a lot older than us and were dressed like normal people, no studded leather jackets with A.C.A.B. on the back.

There was the Teddy Boy or two around who gave us a stare and carried on their Friday night as if we were only there for the one night and maybe had got lost and would never grace their doorstep again. We had heard about someone called Abbo who was a Forest fan (like us) and someone not to throw down the gauntlet to, but we never dared to have eye-to-eye contact for more than a millisecond with anyone.

The music was just what we wanted, plenty of Soul and Motown, but we decided not to dance around the handbags just yet, we more or less cased the joint. We didn't know a soul in there but the beer gave us some confidence that we should be there, a part of the Grey Topper! Older youths had bragged about how many good times they had there and we were a part of that scene now.

We had left the apron strings of Church Hall youth clubs with the bottles of Coca Cola. We felt at home until I watched Pud go across the dance floor wearing the Dr Marten's boots and realised we were the only two lads in the whole place wearing ex-Skinhead attire and we stood out a mile. Luckily our hair had now grown and we classed ourselves as Smoothies rather than Skins. The regulars didn't take us seriously and we got along fine for the next few Friday nights. It was our 'in' place now.

Then about a month later, after Pud had a go at someone for dancing with his 'bird', he looked furtively across at the locals (all bigger and older than us) staring at us and we realised we were out of our depth.

He was escorted to the toilets by a bloke on each arm, his feet off the ground as he went by me. With beer induced confidence I was about to give him assistance when I was also taken by each arm and thoroughly pasted. I looked up to see a fist hit me straight on the nose, followed by a knee, then a few kicks for good measure as I collapsed on the beer soaked dance floor. The bouncers came immediately, one on each arm as they threw me out.

'And don't come back if you're causing trouble again,' they said in a partisan tone.

I learned never to argue first after that, someone could sneeze and I'd have me fists up ready for many a year. Well Pud never got his bird and my loose teeth and bent nose got back to normal after some months keeping my head low.

Still we went back to the Topper of a Friday night and blended in again and saw groups like Mud and Paper Lace who later became top artists.

Ah Mud and Paper Lace now we're talking. But as I continue to go through the local newspapers from 1970-71, looking for the Grey Topper advertisements in the entertainment section, I'm still not coming across many bands that sent the heartbeat racing – The Moon Pennies, New Formula, Rainbow Cottage (or is that an early appearance of George, Bungle and Zippy?) I laugh at the name Pig Boy Charlie Band, it sounds like the band name of some crazed hillbillies out of the film *Deliverance*....

....Later I'm watching Sex Pistols film-maker Julien Temple's brilliant, award winning *Oil City Confidential* about influential pub rockers Dr Feelgood. Their manager Chris Fenwick is just describing their first gig outside of London, off of junction 27 of the M1 in Nottinghamshire at the 'Silk Top Hat Club,' when called the Pig Boy Charlie Band!

My mouth falls open. Surely it's a gig at the Grey Topper he means? I leave messages via Dr Feelgood websites and on the Facebook *Oil City Confidential* page.

I soon receive a reply on the latter that Chris Fenwick would be happy to talk to me, an email is given, then phone numbers are swapped.

Chris Fenwick: We've played hundreds of gigs over the years, so of course you don't remember them all, but this one really stands out. It was our first outside of London. This agent from Southend had booked us this gig up north, well it was north to us.

I remember thinking it was called something like the 'great top hat club' as there was neon sign with a top hat on outside. I felt affinity with Jacksdale, it being a pit village as - when I was starting out in acting as a young lad - I was given the part in a recruitment film for kids going into mining industry.

We weren't called Dr Feelgood then, our name was the Pigboy Charlie Band, I became their manager after getting the sack from the band when we were a jug band and I played the jugs. We drove up the M1 to the Grey Topper in a converted ambulance we used as a tour bus back then, we called it the 'pig bus.'

In the band then was Lee Brilleux on vocals, Sparko on bass and I think Billy Coyle.

I recall the club being a stereotypical northern working man's club with a glittery backdrop. There was these stairs that came down into the club at the far end and onto the stage, and I remember Lee Brilleaux making his entrance down these in his gig gear, denim jacket, gloves and putting on a great show, and the DJ – a well seasoned one as I recall – taking Lee in and saying something like 'Fookin ell you've got a star there mate.'

We all took it very serious, this was our big chance and when the gig went down well we thought we'd arrived.

And we had, we've never looked back, the band quickly

evolved into Dr Feelgood and we were selling out places. We've been on the road ever since. Julien Temple's film about us *Oil City Confidential* has sent interest in us rocketing again, we're booked up solid for the next 18 months.

This is a great coincidence you getting in touch and has sparked some great memories and made me realise that next year it will be 40 years from the Grey Topper gig and that's how long I've been in management!

So there you have it, an early incarnation of Dr Feelgood, playing stripped back, high energy rock 'n' roll, starting to lay down the foundations for punk, going on to have an influence on The Clash, Sex Pistols, The Ramones and Blondie and it started at the Grey Topper in 1971!

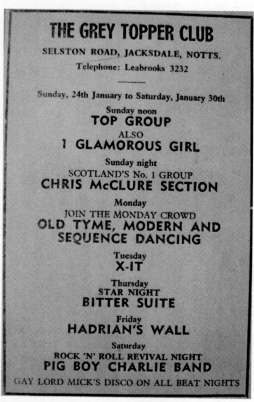

Gay Lord Mick knew a good rock 'n' roll band when he saw one. Wonder who the 'top group' were and wonder if they were upstaged by 1 glamorous girl?

BABYLON'S BURNING 5

July 1979

In the news –

Police unveil new devices to catch speeding motorists 'weapon No.1' The Truvelo Electronic vehicle speed calculator. – 'Weapon No.2' the Muniquip detection device which resembles a hair dryer. 'This must be embarrassing for our butch bobbies' comments a local paper.

Daredevil Eddie Kid is bringing his show to Sutton.

Films of the time *The First Great Train Robbery*. This is not true, that happened in Ironville, the tough neighbouring village to Jacksdale. In the Victorian days Ironvillains blocked the railway line between the two villages to plunder a goods train.

A Grundig Video is £599 and a Hitachi Hi-Fi £369. We look at them longingly in the window of the CO-OP in Jacksdale. A few days later Ironvillains ram raid the place.

A judge gives a Selston man a 2 year suspended jail sentence for GBH after a fight at the Grey Topper. He pleads he didn't know what he was doing as he'd drank 16 pints.

'Skegby Miner's Welfare – comedienne Olga Graham could be a pleasant surprise.

Huthwaite Victoria – customers will be let left Breathless and Envy Street are another highly rated group.'

Roy take a look at the Grey Topper ad below you, at who's on there this month, they just might be worth mentioning. The Simple Minds (misspelled in the local press ad as Simple Minos), come the 80's five of their albums will enter the chart at No.1, 30 million record sales worldwide, 'Belfast Child' will top the singles chart....

'Sutton Social – A touch of country and western with Driftin Country.'

Go on, catch the B7 down to Jacksdale, The Pretenders are back, come the end of the year they'll have the first of three No.1's.....

'There's a scoop for the Unwin Road Social Club with Carl Clayton and Ann, this versatile duo have appeared at all the major clubs in the country so don't be late'

Never mind Roy.

At school us mini punks were listening in awe to a lad about his nights in the Grey Topper. Being 16 he could get in there. He'd just put up a huge *Never Mind The Bollocks, Here's The Sex Pistols* poster on the wall of our form room. Then in walked a teacher and, much to the annoyance of the Topper lad, taped a blank white piece of paper over the word 'bollocks.'

'Aw sir what yuh doin?'

'I'm not having that on display in my form room.'

'Why not? It looks stupid nah. Never Mind the blank.'

'He, he never mind the blankety blank,' chirped up one cheeky lad. 'Who d'yuh think you are, Terry Wogan? He, he.'

The Topper lad pushed him firmly in the shoulder, and pointed a threatening finger. 'You're dead in playground.'

'Never mind the blank generation,' put in the teacher.

'What's wrong wi bollocks anyroad?'

'We can't have profanity in school Michael, you know that. So stop saying it.'

'What's profanity?'

'Swearing.'

'Bollocks aint swearing.'

'Michael last warning, you know damn well it is so stop showing off.'

'No, that's were yuh wrong see, it were on *Midlands Today* a year back. Virgin Records in Nottingham put a load of Never mind the Bollocks' –

'Right that's it detention,' interrupted the teacher.

'No yuh can't, I've done nowt, hear me out see. They put loads of the albums in the window, the council or police ordered them to remove em, they refused and were taken to court. Johnny Rotten turned up and they got this English professor to prove bollocks' –

'Another detention.'

'It's legal, this professor said it wer an Anglo Saxon word meaning small balls.'

'Have you got small balls sir?' asked a girl.

The teacher was now red. 'I don't care, it's swearing in my book.'

'Yuh wrong, judge agreed and Johnny Rotten sprung out of court shouting bollocks is legal' –

'Treble detention.'

'Yeah he ran dahn street going up to people saying bollocks, bollocks –'

'Detention.'

'Bollocks.'

'There's another.'

'Bollocks, bollocks, bollocks is legal.'

'Headmaster now.'

There'd been a resurgence in the popularity of the Sex Pistols in 1979, first with the tragic death of Sid Vicious, at the age of 21, from a drugs overdose while on bail for the alleged murder of his girlfriend Nancy Spungen, securing his place as a rock 'n' roll legend.

Then following the release of Julien Temple's Sex Pistols film *The Great Rock 'n' Roll Swindle,* which produced an album and a rash of Rotten-free singles.

Spike: When we went to see that we were all pogoing on the stage in front of the screen. I went to punch this bloke on screen who was moaning about the Sex Pistols, what I didn't know was that there was this trench in-between the stage and the screen and fell down there and couldn't get out, then Feff, Marsy and Mick and a few more fell in as well.

Tink: We used to hang about with 'celebrity punk' Pat Mark when we went down London around then. He was one of the main punks down there then. He was wearing these checked colour trousers and had 'Sid Vicious' cut into the back of his hair.

Mick Clark: We went to his squat, he had Sid's clothes that his mum had given him, leather jacket, belt and jeans.

Tink: The jeans still had his or someone else's bloodstains on them, they were like holy relics to us.

Mick Clark: Yeah and he let us try them on!

Feff: Pat Mark became Toyah's minder. I knew him then. Once I'd been mugged on Kings Road and when he heard about it he sent some youths looking for them for me.

Mick Clark: He always challenged Spike to an arm wrestle whenever they met. I became good mates with him and for a very short while I helped him run the Sid Vicious fan club.

The Sex Pistols didn't entertain my dad's ears either. One day I was in my bedroom listening to the track 'Holidays in the Sun' from the album *Never Mind the Bollocks*,

'Now I got a reason..now I got a reason…now I got a reason, and I'm still waiting,' sang Johnny Rotten, when Dad stuck his head around the door.

'I got a reason as well, to turn the bloody thing off. What's the problem with this lot? What they trying to prove? It's just a racket. I can stick a Bing Crosby record on, go t'top of garden and still hear every word he sings. Yuh can't do that with these bloody punk groups,' Dad lectured me.

I'd just returned from a family holiday in Great Yarmouth where I purchased a 'Sid Vicious Lives' t-shirt. This girl who I fancy, Tracy, seems suitably impressed with my attire.

'So you're a punk then?'

'Yeah,' I reply nonchalantly and gob on her shoe.

'Cool!'

We spend quite a bit of time hanging round together with her best friend Joanne Forsdyke and her brother Nigel. Many happy hours in our secret den, which as dens go is of the deluxe variety as it's a fully furnished house. It's next door to the Forsdyke's and Nigel explains that an old woman lived there, then about three years ago she went to visit a sister in London and never came back.

It's like the Mary Celeste as we sneak in through a back window, breakfast things are still on the table, piles of letters in front of the door, an old fashioned television and radio. The girls try on mothballed coats and flowery hats, everything just as she left it, except spiders have built cable cars from cakes to book shelves. It's magical, like *Great Expectations*. We expect to see the old lady any minute in a rocking chair wearing a decrepit wedding dress.

We're playing hide and seek one day. Tracy and me hide in the outside toilet, she holds my hand, then kisses me. It's the most magical moment in this young punks life....

A week later she was going out with a smelly greb. The most soul-destroying thing was, they pass me in the street and Tracy doesn't even acknowledge me. He does, he gobs on my shoe.

*

There's rumblings among the residents about the escalating trouble after nights at the Topper and punks invading the place.

Tink: My mum had the hairdressers across the road. One morning my dad went down to open up and clean the place. As he approached the outside toilet he could see these spikes sticking out of the door. There was these two punks from London asleep in there.

My dad comes home from work moaning that when he goes down the gitty to catch the bus for his night shift at work, he can't get on because it's crammed with youths heading for the Topper. If he does squeeze on they take the piss out of his pac-a-mac.

'Bloody cheeky gits said it would look punk if they tore a few holes in it and add chains.'

Two flat-capped old timers stop and examine the poster on the Topper billboard.

'Simple Minds Arthur, see it, Simple bloody minds?'

'Ahh.'

'That just about ses it all, Simple bloody minds.'

'Appen.'

'Simple minds for simpletons.'

'Ahh.'

Jim Kerr's - Lou Reed, Bowie and Roxy Music influenced, Scottish New Wave rockers Simple Minds played the Grey Topper on Friday the 13th of July 1979. Even though they'd appeared on the influential *Old Grey Whistle Test* they were still years from achieving their ambitions. Debut single 'Life In a Day' and follow up 'Chelsea Girl' barely dented the Top 100. Hence only a handful of people witnessing their gig at the Topper. One set of friends however would be impressed enough to go and form their own band.

Steve Hovington - B-Movie: I remember seeing Simple Minds there. It was amazing, like a private gig. We were the audience!

Exactly six years later, on July 13th 1985, the Simple Minds would take to the stage in front of 90,000 people at the JFK Stadium, Philadelphia, as part of the biggest worldwide live music event in history, Live Aid.

They performed 'Ghostdancing', 'Don't You Forget About Me' and 'Promised You A Miracle.' They must have thought that's what had happened if they realised that on that very night in 1979 they were on the stage in front of a small mob of baying punks in a Nottinghamshire pit village.

The next but one (the one being Bowie) act on after the Simple Minds at Live Aid, Philadelphia were The Pretenders. As they had been at the Grey Topper in 1979, just two days later.

It's the only gig I ever went to at the Topper, so to speak. I'd bought their single 'Kid' the day before and was sat on the wall as they turned up – in a proper tour bus – to try and get a glimpse of the band. That night me and a few friends stood outside the Topper to listen best we could to the gig.

Their first gig - back in March at the Topper – had gone well, even though the crowd had been small. Spike and the lads met Chrissie Hynde later and she chatted happily away to them. Now the place had become an infamous punk venue, rammed to the rafters, sporadic fights kicking off and –

Tink: It was like snow, a hailstorm, all this gob flying through the air showering the band.

Chrissie Hynde had been there at the inception of punk. Arriving in London from Ohio, USA with her guitar in the mid 1970's, desperate to be part of the punk movement and form her own band. She found herself a job working in Vivienne Westwood's Sex Shop on the King's Road selling punk clothes. Soon she was sharing squats with the Sex Pistols, trying to teach Johnny Rotten how to play the guitar and paying Sid Vicious to marry her so she could stay in England when her visa ran out.

Now three years on, at the Topper, Chrissie Hynde was confronted by a mob of Sid Vicious clones - black spiky hair, leather jackets, right down to his trademark padlock and chain, like the one she'd given him. Worst of all they'd not only adopted his image but also the ugly attitude of punk, which Vicious had in large part created.

Feff: She'd just started singing 'Stop Your Sobbing' when the spit stated flying again. She suddenly changed the lyrics to 'You gotta stop gobbing now, yeah, yeah stop it, stop it!' But it continued so they stopped playing. The guitarist took the mike and said 'Look we're not a punk band, if you don't stop gobbing we're walking off stage.' It quietened down then and they finished their set.

Chrissie Hynde and Jim Kerr were married in 1984. I wonder if they ever reminisced about that weekend, no not Live Aid, the Grey Topper?

From the nightmare of Friday the 13th in a tough old mining village – where they can't even get your name right - playing to a handful of people.
To exactly 6 years on being a multi-million record selling group, playing one of the biggest gigs in history – to a crowd of over 90,000 in the J.F.K. Stadium and a worldwide TV audience of billions. Other one-time Topper acts sharing Simple Minos fate that day – The Pretenders, Judas Priest, Adam Ant and Ultravox.

This Charming Man

Another artist who's Brylcreem Elvis quiff, cheesy smile and denims were all over the pages of 80's *Smash Hits* was Shakin' Stevens. But many years before he was becoming one of the best selling artists of that decade with a string of number 1's and attacking Richard Madeley live on TV, he and his band The Sunsets were doing the northern club circuit and at the Grey Topper attacking an old woman's piano.

Ally Key: Someone had kicked in his green door and pinched his piano before the gig.

'There's no way I can go on without a piano,' Shaky told us.

'I know what, old Mrs Smithurst across the road has a piano, perhaps I can talk her into lending us that,' I told him.

It was this real grand old thing that had belonged to her mother, covered in candelabras and an aspidistra plant, but it was our only chance of getting the gig on.

She took some talking round. 'It's not for them rockers is it?'

'No, no, we're having an old time sing-a-long for pensioners,' I explained my nose growing by the minute.

'Ok then but I want it back in same condition as it is now.'

'Promise.'

Shakin' wasn't too impressed but said it would have to do. I then had to go somewhere. My mouth dropped in horror when I got back. Shakin' had stripped it down to get it like he wanted to.

Worse was to come when the gig got underway. Talk about Shakin' his hips, he knocked bloody hell out of this piano, then sprung up on top of it to gyrate. I'd got my head in my hands thinking bloody hell, thoughts of a roller pin around the head. We had to stay up to two in the morning putting it back together, polishing candelabras and gluing keys back.

You couldn't leave anything lying around outside the Topper. Alf was always having to buy his lads Brian and Mark new bikes. They kept leaving them around the back of the club and there was always someone leaving the club, who'd missed the last bus home, pinching them.

*

At least Shakin' Stevens survived the loss of his piano, went on with the show and eventually made it to superstardom. For another hard up early 70's band the loss of their equipment at the Topper apparently lead to their demise.

I found the following on a website called 'Manchester Beat - the music scene of the 60's' -

'My Hampshire based band formed in 1967, secured a two month long residency with Paul Vonk in West Germany in 1972.

The first, in April, was at the Hilly-Billy Tanzbar in a town called Kitzingen, near Wurzburg. The second, in August, was in Frankfurt at the Maxim Bar, 8pm-3am every night.

After the second engagement we changed our name from Technicolor Dream to SHOP (our surnames were Syrad, Hewson, Owens, Parks), and returned to England and auditioned successfully for the Barry Collins agency in Southend. We toured the country, including supporting Billy J. Kramer at the Yarborough Club in Doncaster, from September 72 until Jan 73 when equipment stolen from our van after a gig at the Grey Topper Club in Nottinghamshire speeded up our demise. '

Poor bastard, typical Topper. I'll bet there's days now when stuck in some mind numbing job, they start day dreaming back to the salad days of their youth, free and single in a pop group with potential. 'I could have been someone, we could have been contenders, if it hadn't been for those thieving bastards in Jacksdale. I'll have my revenge one day, if I can find the bloody place.'

I contact the webmaster of the site to find out who they were and if he has contact details. He replies that someone just posted the message and no one he knows had heard of the groups SHOP or Technicolor Dream.

*

Ally Key, who told me the Shakin' Stevens story, was the village milkman and one the best friends of Grey Topper owner Alf Hyslop and used to help him run the club.

I was looking forward to meeting him again as I remember him with affection. He'd call in at ours on Saturday mornings to collect the milk money and would end up chatting to my parents for twenty minutes, we'd gather around to hear this charming man, always with a smile on his face and tale to tell.

Ally Key: I'd never get done Saturday mornings, I'd spend so long chatting to people that by the time I'd done it was getting dark and I'd have to be off out on the milk round or down the Topper.

It's a hot summer day when I find Ally at the top of his garden in the last of a long line of ramshackle sheds. He's in his 80's now but looks fit and healthy and wearing a bandanna makes him look like a veteran *Easy Rider*. He's working on his vintage Morris car. Still quick to spot a business opportunity.

Ally: This guy who runs a wedding company came to see it. He says if I can get it on the road again he'll pay me £180 a time to hire it out for weddings.

I ask him how Alf came to own and run the Grey Topper.

Ally: He started an open cast coal business and made a small fortune. We used to go to this club that had live bands and cabaret on. We'd spend a fortune there, Alf drank pink champagne. I turned to him and said. 'Why not open your own club, then not only will alcohol and entertainment be free but you'll make money out of it.

They'd looked at many old cinemas in the area before settling on the empty Picture Palace at Jacksdale. They rebuilt it, then they had to attract customers.

Ally: At first we had these leaflets printed and distributed them to the factories and pits in the area. We thought a good idea would be to charge men, but let women in for free so we put – COME TO THE GREY TOPPER – 200 COCKS AND HENS LAID FREE.

It was a cabaret club to begin with, but although it initially did well, it started to die off when the novelty of being a new club had started to wear off, it was no different from any other entertainment on offer in the area. So thoughts turned to making it a live music venue and try and attract bigger bands. That's what Alf dreamed of anyway.

Like a real life *Field Of Dreams*?

Ally: Yeah it was, he built it and they came, Freddie and the Dreamers, Marty Wilde, Bobby Vee, Billy Fury, Del Shannon, The Merseybeats, Swinging Blue Jeans, Hermin's Hermits, Gerry and the Pacemakers.

I heard Billy Haley played there? Did you meet him? Ally frowns.

Ally: Oh yeah, turned out to be the most expensive bloody handshake of my life. We'd booked him for £700 and only made £300. Couldn't wait to say see yuh later alligator. When we booked Bill Haley and the Comets we thought this is it, everyone will hear about the Grey Topper now, home to the rock 'n' roll greats. He played to about 20 people!

It was our fault though, we made it all ticket and Alf

announced 'If you haven't got a ticket for this one don't bother showing up.' It should have been pay on the door. Then there was the weather. It was terrible, snow and ice and you know what its like down there, you can't get in or out of the bloody place in bad weather.

Great times though?

Ally: I have to pinch myself at times, when I look back and think, there was me a humble milkman in a pit village rubbing shoulders with famous pop stars.

One time we had a dinner party with Errol Brown from Hot Chocolate and Screaming Lord Sutch. It was like the United Nations mixed with the mad hatters tea party. Errol's wife was Chinese, Screaming Lord Sutch's French, Alf was a Geordie and Emma Scottish.

Ally: I remember asking Screaming Lord Sutch why he did all this Monster Raving Loony Party stuff when he knew he was bound to lose the deposit.

'Best publicity in the World Ally and I get up the noses of the stuffy politicians.'

I told Errol Brown he'd never get anywhere playing the music he did. Years later he sent me a postcard from some tropical island with millions of hit records sold.

What about the punk years?

Ally: It was just the music of the time, we always went with the flow with what the kids wanted, so that's what we gave them. They packed the place out, but we didn't realise how much trouble it would bring. We didn't mind things like them throwing beer all over each other. They could do what they liked with it as long as they'd bought it.

All I was concerned with at first was the new floor. Alf had just had it put down, it was made up of all these wooden blocks. The company who laid it gave us advice on how to look after it. I used to polish it regularly and they recommended this powder. Only I must have put down too much, the disco dancers were sliding all over the place, there were a few John Travoltas that split their trousers. Then bloody punks started pogoing up and down and chucking beer all over it and I'm going 'Oooh me floor, me floor.'

We tried to book the Sex Pistols once, but I reckon it was just before they split, no one else wanted them but we did.

Summer of 79

'Sunday's rather special at the Sutton Social as one of my favourite duos, the fabulous Mel Douglas Duo appear. Hear them sing 'Bright Eyes' and I'm sure you will agree it will be a night to remember.'

Roy, don't be afraid of the punks, come on down to the Jacksdale, it may be worth your while. Adam's bringing his Ants to the Topper, they've potential, honest, come the 80's they'll have ten Top 10 singles three of which will reach No.1....

'The Sunday show at Sutton Labour club goes to brilliant vent act Tony Adams and Grandad who are an absolute must.'

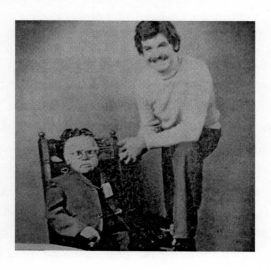

In the news -

North Notts mining record. 1800 men produced the highest weekly tonnage of coal ever. 15 mines produced 285,375 tonnes.

Local man's chicken lays unusual egg.

Outrage from residents over 'hooligans skateboarding over graves.' The kids appeal for a skateboard park.

The magnetic brilliance of Seve Ballesteros at getting a ball in a hole with a stick made golf 'cool' for a week or two. So our gang chipped in to buy a driver from a jumble sale, tucked our jeans into our football socks, donned our grandad's flat caps and headed for our golf course, which in our case was the cattle field at the edge of the estate. The winner of the 'Palmerston Street Open' was the one who could land the golf ball in a cowpat from fifty yards. The loser, and this was usually me, had to retrieve the ball and get the Juicy Jims in from the top shop. Bring on the football season, getting a bag of wind into a net was something I was good at, and anyway we all knew that golf was too elitist and expensive for oiks like us to become superstars of the game.

Back to playing football on the rec, that was a working class sport played by working class kids. Forest star striker Tony Woodcock came from Eastwood, the mining town just up the road. He'd been spotted playing for Priory Celtic too, a team which me and many of my mates played for, so maybe just maybe we could make it too?

Working class kids could also dream of being rock stars now as well, punk had showed us that. You no longer needed to be able to play the guitar like Eric Clapton, read music or crawl to major record labels. Do it yourself, just put 3 chords together, bash out a tune whilst venting your feelings, easy.

With this in mind and inspired by the punk bands on at the Topper, Spike and the lads decided to form their own band.

Spike: There was me, Mick Clark, Feff and Cork, we called ourselves Submission or Vicious Kids, something like that and painted it on our leather jackets next to the legend 'Topper Punks.' Alf had a drum kit he leant us and we bought a guitar, bass, amps and stuff and painted this big banner.

We rehearsed on the Topper stage, there was all these people watching us Sunday dinnertime, but we were crap, talk about three chords we couldn't do two.

Mick Clark: Cork was useless on the guitar, every time he tried to play something he'd break a string.

Spike: As soon as the pumps came on and everyone was getting pissed we thought fuck it, let's go and have some beer. Worst was to come, Alf's daughter came talking to us with this pet puppy Alf had given her, we gave it some beer, got it pissed, Yvonne went mad and we got barred, again, we were always getting barred.

We'd got pissed in other pubs that night and were sat back in my kitchen, when the Topper doorman Malc burst in, as pissed as us, swaying about. He was trying to be all-serious but his flies were undone and his pants sticking out, so we couldn't stop laughing. 'Nah, nah, let me tell yuh, all your gears all over street, that's raight, your gears all over street, there's no band.'

He was right they'd chucked our stuff into the road. That was the end of the Vicious White Kids.

The following Sunday Adam brought down his Ants to show the Vicious White Kids how it should be done. Well as soon as their gear was set up.

Feff: It was real funny. Alf's lads Brian and Mark and their mates had just put down jumpers for goalposts in the Topper car park and got their football match underway, when Adam and the Ants showed up in their tour van. All these kids wouldn't let them by to park up and unload their gear until a winning goal had been scored. I reckon the band joined in though.

Mick Clark: Adam and the Ants were very special, and their travelling support looked like a Seditionaries catwalk show. I was humbled beyond belief by their dress sense, humbled but in heaven. I'd seen the Ants before at Nottingham and I thought they were fantastic.

Stuart Goddard was part of the punk scene from the very beginning. The first band he was in - playing bass - was called Bazooka Joe.

Eddie – The Vibrators: I was their roadie, drove the van for them. Later Eddie later…

They were the main act at St Martins College of Art when the Sex Pistols made their debut and changed the face of rock music forever in November 1975. Later Stuart Goddard changed his name to Adam Ant and formed his own band. Jordan from

Sex became their manager. Their sound was dark, with punk riffs and elements of glam rock. And Adam was far from being a prince charming at the time, his image was fetish and sadomasochistic influenced as he explained at the time –

'I'm not personally into S&M, I mean I never smacked the arse of anybody. It's the power, it's the imagery. There's a certain imagery involved with that which I find magnetic. It's not done viciously, if you read S&M mags and spank mags or anything like that, it's done with an essence of humour, wardress and stuff, that just appeals to my imagination.'

This was still very much the sound and image of the group when they played the Grey Topper in 1979 as part of the 'Zerox' tour. They must have thought they were on the verge of the breakthrough when they received the dates for that tour – MANCHESTER – THE FACTORY, LIVERPOOL – ERIC'S, LONDON – LYCEUM and, oh, Jacksdale – Grey Topper?

Tink: Adam looked amazing, he had this snake skin face paint, bondage trousers, a blue kilt and leather jacket.

Spike: Yeah but he didn't have the jacket for long did he, we nicked it. He was trying to get it back but there was no way. Later I saw him in the toilet with this blue marker pen scrawling 'I hate Topper punks' on the wall.

Feff: Yeah that was there for years.

Spike: I was wearing his jacket a few weeks later when we went down London. We ended up going down the Mall to Buckingham Palace. I climbed to the top of the gates. There's a photo somewhere, me with blonde spiky hair, bondage trousers, wearing Adam Ants jacket, hanging from the palace gates giving two fingers to the Queen.

Feff: It was a great gig.

Mick Clark: They didn't seem to like the Topper and played indifferently as I remember it. They wrote on the toilet wall about hating the Grey Topper, but I loved them anyway. I remember talking to Adam in the lounge bar and he was a really decent and friendly guy. His mood changed though and rumour has it that someone nicked his jacket - don't know if that's true or not but something put him in a bad mood during the performance.

Tink: Henny threw a pint at Adam, he dodged it but was fuming, he stopped the band and wanted to take Henny on.

Still success eluded Adam, so he paid Sex Pistol's manager Malcolm McLaren £1000 to be an image consultant. Following his advice Adam adopted a swashbuckling pirate look, combined with Native American imagery and with a sound that incorporated African-inspired drumming, dubbed 'Burundi Beat.' The first teen idol of the 1980's was born and millions of record sales followed.

30 years on....Adam Ant had been off the music radar for years. Suffering from mental illness, he'd been in and out of psychiatric hospital many times. The tabloid newspapers had a field day at the dramatic fall of 'Prince Charming'. Especially when suffering from another bout of manic depression, that had plagued him all his adult life, he burst into a pub – wearing a combat jacket, leather trousers, shades and a white cowboy hat - and threatened several people with an imitation firearm.

A little while later he made a documentary *The Madness Of Prince Charming* and appeared lucid as he spoke about his illness, showing signs that he was in recovery. Now he was back, on stage performing, talking of going back into the studio to record new material, and for the release of his autobiography *Stand And Deliver*, a best of CD collection and DVD. I saw - on one of his dedicated fans web sites - that he was to do a book signing in Waterstones, Manchester and decided it was worth taking the opportunity to meet him and see if he can remember the gig at the Grey Topper.

It's a Tuesday when I catch the train on up there. He's not due to appear until 5.00pm, I'm there in the city at 12.00pm. With plenty of time on my hands (I do pop over to Waterstones at intervals in the afternoon to check there's not masses of old Ants starting to queue) I wander around the city and go to Urbis 'the museum of urban life.' There's often something to do with the music scene on display (today it's The Smiths).

The last time I went to Urbis there was a punk exhibition on. Loads of original clothes designed by Vivien Westwood in the 1970's as worn by the Sex Pistols, handwritten lyrics by Johnny Rotten and Sid Vicious (after the Sex Pistols) and interactive stuff about the Manchester music scene.

There were these two middle-aged women looking around, who must have been original punks and they still dressed as they would have done in the late 1970's – one had blue spiky hair the other pink, leopard skin skirts, fishnet stockings and leather jackets. I was wondering if they had teenage daughters and what their reaction would be?

'Mum, you're not going out dressed like that!'

Or how embarrassed they'd be if they came home with mates or boyfriends to find their mum and mate pogoing around the room to *Never Mind the Bollocks here's the Sex Pistols*. Telling her to take that crap off so she and her friends can listen to Eminem.

The queue in Waterstones has started to form, it's 3.30 pm, still an hour and half until Prince Charming arrives. I buy his autobiography and eagerly turn to the index and the listings under G....no Grey Topper. What about Jacksdale....nothing. So I turn to the pages linked to 'Zerox.' There's only three and just a paragraph covering the tour. All he says is that they did 15 dates on the tour and that a sold out one at the Lyceum in London helped them get a £100,000 record deal with Polydor.

Disappointed I take my place in the queue, about 50 yards from the front. An hour later, the queue stretches the length of the huge shop and back again and out the door. There is a spattering of young indie, goth and punk types but it's mainly middle-aged people, middle-aged punks, one thirty-something Adam complete with *Kings of the Wild Frontier* get-up and white war paint across his nose. Several have old Ants tour t-shirts. I'm looking for one with the 'Zerox' tour, but don't spot any, I do see an Indian type badge that I remember my brother painting way back in 1981. All these with this type of t-shirt seem to know each other as they exchange handshakes and smiles and excitedly chat about the day they've been waiting for so long.

I decide it would be of interest - and potentially beneficial - to chat to people in the queue.

'Did you ever see them live?' I ask the thirty-something chap in front of me.

'Wha...wha?' He replies, wild stare on his face, sweating profusely, shaking a little, hugging the autobiography tightly, clutching something in his pocket tightly. As I look on the bookshelves, that we're standing next to, I see copies of *The Catcher In The Rye* and wonder if it's a gun he's hiding. Have I placed myself next to the Mark Chapman of the Ant world? He certainly looks perturbed so I leave it.

Mostly the queue is full of women. There's a large rotund woman at the other side of me. She dragged her adolescent son along. He's full of excitement, slumped on the floor, baseball hat pulled down over above his eyes, playing a Gameboy. I can't understand why she's bothered bringing him, then he inspects the three copies of *Stand and Deliver* in the bag resting on his legs.

'Are ya really sure we'll get something for these on Ebay? Not exactly 50 Cent is he?' He asks his mum.

She's too busy chatting to her female friend about the old times.

'I wet myself when I saw him in concert once,' I hear her tell her friend, a little too loudly, her son has heard.

'Mummmm! Gross!' He pulls his cap firmly down over his eyes and lowers his head.

'Adam, you don't understand,' she retorts.

Adam? He couldn't have been born until well into the 1990's, long after Adam's star had faded. Was her devotion so great that she'd still named her son after her teenage idol? Then she nearly passes out when a shop assistant lets it slip that he'll be emerging from the lift door about 10 yards back and walking straight past us. I'm hoping she doesn't want to remove her huge pissed stained knickers to throw at him.

Then it's announced he'll be half an hour late as they're stuck in traffic driving up from Birmingham. Groans all round, the crazy ant guy in front of me is muttering to himself.

'No, no, this is my day.'

Adam Ant finally steps out of the lift with minder and management at 5.35 pm. I'm expecting cheers, whoops and applause as I'd read on an Ant website that that was the reaction

81

at a book signing in London a few days before, but there's just excited chatter and the flashing of camera bulbs. Guess Northerners have a higher adulation threshold than Southern softies. This is, after all, a city that's had more than it's fair share of pop icons and George Best. I just mange to get a shot of his minder's shoulder with my digital camera as they walk by.

The queue moves slowly, even though the small Jack Russell of a woman at Adam's side, who appears to be in charge of things, snaps at people to move on if they've taken up more than a minute of Ant's time, no fault on his part and I notice he looks a bit annoyed by this himself.

Crazy ant in front of me finally gets his big moment. He bends down to the seated 80's pop star, and juts his head at him several times. A wave of panic sweeps through me, from where I'm stood it looks like crazy ant is head-butting Adam. Oh shit! Why doesn't someone stop him? Why don't the Waterstones bounces - stood 10 yards away - pile in, why isn't the Jack Russell biting his ankles? I'm thinking.

Oh and now he's reaching into his pocket, the gun, I'm preparing myself to rugby tackle him, well dive under the table of cookbooks more like, when crazy ant pulls out a faded C60, C90 audio cassette tape and thrusts it at Adam. I then realise that the head movements are attributed to a machine gun verbal delivery, having to say everything he always wanted to say to his idol in a minute. The tape is probably some demo from some Ant influenced band he was in eons ago, that, in crazy ants mind, should have been contenders if only the record companies had taken the time to listen to it in 1981, there's still hope, Adam will hear its potential. Sure he will.

Soon I find myself getting into the same boat as crazy ant, blurting out what I want to say as the clock ticks down. I had planned to get his attention by asking him if he'd write 'To Spike, where's my jacket? Adam Ant,' inside the front cover of *Stand and Deliver*. But as we queued a Waterstones employee had come down the line to instruct us that there would be no personal dedications, just Adam's elaborate signature. So off I go, feeling like Spud in *Trainspotting* during his job interview high on speed.

'Hi Adam – on the Zerox tour in 1979 – you played here at the Factory' A semblance of a nod from Adam there – 'Liverpool Eric's' – same reaction – 'London Lyceum' same slight reaction – 'but what about a Notts mining village called Jacksdale – a venue called the Grey Topper?????' – wide eyed bemusement from Adam, no words he utters and Jack Russell is scowling at me, the clocks ticking as loud as the one in *Countdown* in my head. 'Kids in the car park playing football, jumpers for goal posts (oh fuck can't believe I said that) when you showed up' – silence, wider eyes – 'my mate nicked your leather jacket?' – mouth slightly open, a quizzically stare – then Jack Russell intervenes and indicates it's time to move on.

In readiness for this outcome I'd put everything about the Topper project in an A4 envelope. I try to hand this to Adam but Jack Russell snatches it from my hand and plonks it down on a pile of other fans letters.

'It's in there, see if the Grey Topper's in your diary (I know he's kept a diary since 1977). Thanks for playing a pit village, punk did change people,' I say with a smile as I walk away. There's a hint of a smile on Adam Ant's face too as I walk away, but he still looks a little confused and doesn't speak.

I start reading his autobiography on the train home and can't put it down over the next few days. I find it incredibly sad when he reveals the extent of his mental health and the depressing state it's left him in since the new millennium.

I'm hoping he can get the confidence back to get back up on stage again, as performing live used to give him a bigger buzz and lift his spirits more than anything (apart from sex, he had a lot of that of course) Not on some 80's nostalgia tour, they'd just be expecting to see some ageing dandy highwayman, a pantomime pop star like he became.

I'm thinking about the likes of The Vibrators, UK Subs

Charlie Harper, The Rolling Stones and Lemmy (of course). Team up with 'Zerox' Ant's Dave Barbe, Andy Warren, with Marco on guitar (Matthew Ashman died of diabetes aged 35 in 1998) and get back to pure rock 'n' roll and his punk roots. Maybe that's some of the medication he needs?*

In May 2010 it was reported in the press that Adam Ant was admitted to the Chelsea and Westminster Hospital after being sectioned under the mental health act. He later turns up to do a gig at the Monster Raving Loony Party's conference, and says he would like to join them.

---

*Stop Press: Adam Ant did get back to his punk roots live, in Jan 2011 he performed early Ants sounds on stage at the 100 Club as part of the campaign to save the famous music venue from closure. This was part of his 'The Good, The Mad and The Lovely World Tour of London.'

Another One Bites The Dust

Over the rooftops in the distance, like some huge, futuristic, cyborg dinosaur, I could see the yellow crane devouring its victim. I quickly grab my camera and headed in the vicinity of the Picture Palace.

A crowd has gathered, many sad that any final chance of another village landmark being saved from extinction is now gone.

'It could have been turned into a sports and entertainment centre,' one comments.

'We had some great times in there didn't we?' says one man nudging another.

'Ssshhh wife's here,' he replies a wry smile on his face.

All but the façade is now rubble. There's hope the letters chiselled into the plaster that make up 'JACKSDALE PICTURE PALACE,' can be saved. The foreman says he's instructed the crane operator to take his time and try his best to preserve them.

In fact the foreman has promised to put one of the letters aside for me if they can.

They were pretty amazed – stood outside the chippy at dinnertime - when I told them the history of the place and famous bands that played there. Until a blonde, in skimpy shorts and bikini top, walks by. I then might as well be talking to what's left of the Topper perimeter wall then as wolf whistles ring out.

Yeah, there's no sentiment for this old building there. Even though at first the crane driver is as good as his word and successfully manages to remove a section that spells 'ACE' (oh would so have loved to have had that), his next effort clumsily knocks the letters smashing to the ground and he gives up. It's a Friday and they can't wait for the place to bite the dust, finish early, collect their wages for a job well done and be out on the piss.

I'm out on the piss with my mates as well later that night up Ripley. So much so that, when I'm dropped off by the taxi in Jacksdale, I just have to go for a P. My new t-shirt gets covered in green stains as I push my through huge conifers and I scratch my arms on the edge of a wire fence. Then twist my ankle stumbling drunkenly over a few bricks.

Oh it's too big and heavy I'll never get that out. I'm thinking. I give another tug and let out a strained noise at the same time.

'Are ya raight yowf?'

I look up and see this couple looking at me with puzzled expressions.

'Yezzz I'm fine, dunt worry about, me,' I reply tripping over a boulder landing on my arse.

'What, er yuh doing like over there?'

'Just want a big P that's all.'

'Appen, but aint yuh got a home t'goo to? Or at least in telephone box if yuv been caught short, you'll break yuh neck over there.'

'I want a big P, if not a P, then a big J or T or an E.'

'Come on duck, he's drugged out his head,' says the woman tugging her partner's arm.

It's no good the letters of JACKSDALE PICTURE PALACE

are on plaster, cemented to lumps of brick. They weigh a ton, there's no way I can lift one – especially in this state – and carry it several hundred yards home. I don't even remember to take a brick. And by the time I next go around there on Tuesday it's all gone.

There's a huge empty space at the end of a street, like the end of a finger had been chopped off and with it a distinctive village fingerprint.

Across the road another huge open space is being turned into a building site, houses are going up. On this spot used to stand the Portland Arms (Hotel). It enjoyed a good relationship and contemplated the vibe at the Topper in its heyday. Gratefully picking up on its overspill. The Portland was decent little music venue in its own right. With many a decent rock and blues and punk act performing there. In fact the field behind it was the location for Jacksdale's own music festival. 'The Earth Dwellers Guide.'

The Earth Dwellers were a strange crowd as they invaded the village once a year on trikes, choppers and rainbow coloured Transit vans to set up tents. They were like a cross between Hell's Angels, new age hippies, acid victims and eco warriors. On certain nights at the Portland during their stay they'd give out trophies to its various members. For what I never figured out, and I wondered why the trophies consisted of a ferret's head stuck on a plaque. The poor little things were Earth dwellers too weren't they?

They'd all then return to the camping ground, light fires, take out pipes - that Gandalph would have been proud of - play strange sounds on all manner of instruments, howl to the moon, before sacrificing one of their young at midnight for the benefit of some unknown god.

Seeing the Grey Topper bite the dust I was even more determined not to allow its story to be buried with it.

'World Cup exit blues, drowned my sorrows again last night, and woke up to a sweltering Monday morning, dehydrated and a jack hammer trying to break out of my skull… and a black eye, a woman I was walking home was as drunk as me and fell on me, banging my head on a path. I ring one time Topper doorman Malc to say I'll be there just after dinner.

'What do you call just after dinner?'

'Err between twelve thirty and one?'

'Mek it twelve yowf.'

It's a quarter to 12.00, I'm still on grapes, water and paracetamol to defeat the hangover and not had a shave and done my ablutions yet.

'Ok,' I reluctantly agree.

I'm in such a rush that I forget to check his address, but know its No.53

I go down the gennel between the terraced houses to No.53 of the first street I come to. The back doors open before I can knock and a grey haired chap emerges.

'Malc?' I offer a handshake.

'Don't care what yuh name is or what yuh sellin, am not interested.'

'No I'm not – '

'Religion, I bloody lost that when England went owt World Cup, so don't sell me that cos I feel on fire, like hell still.'

'Sorry I reckon I'm on the wrong street, I'm looking for ex Topper doorman Malc Fletcher.'

'Malc, hmmm, he lives across street.'

'What 53?'

'Feftee thray, I'm Feftee thray, what sort of topsy turvy street yo live on wi same numbers on same street, nah just across road yowf.'

I go back down the gennel, still not quite sure which house it is, there's an old fellow sat on a wall outside a house watching me suspiciously as I study the front windows of houses wondering what to expect to be on the sill of an ex club doorman; a neon sign, dancing Elvis clock, gold plated knuckle dusters?

He told me on the phone that he has a Scottish and Newcastle statuette from the Topper, perhaps that's on show in the window, but I can't see one. So to be sure I ask the old man.

'Do you know were Malc Fletcher lives?'

The old chap scratches his head.

'No, no ahh dunt need a mac fetching, not rain today yowf,' he says and pulls the knotted handkerchief more tightly over his head, so dunt try to sell me one.'

I go down the gennel directly across from No.53. And come to a gate, a chap is just walking up his garden.

'Alraight,' I call.

He jumps and in the process a few tomatoes roll out of the dish he's carrying and splat on the path in front of him, he treads on one. 'What the?' A yapping Jack Russell appears and nips at the front of my trainer poking through the gate.

I vaguely recognise him – 'Alraight, do you know were Malc lives?'

'That tomato, yowf, was an entry for a vegetable show, one of my best, what the bloody ell yuh on wi sneakin up on folks?'

'Sorry, chap across road seemed to think Malc Fletcher lives.'

'Little Malc?' Topper doorman?'

'Yeah, that's the one.'

'He lives two streets away,' he says pointing over the roof of his house.'

'Oh right, ta, sorry about your tomato.'

'Actually I wer ribbing yuh, that's a reject, if it had been one of my prize ones you'd be a vegetable yuh sen by now. I wer just tekin em to table on deckin to have a ploughman's lunch.'

'Thanks anyway.'

I get back in the car and burn my hands on the sun-scorched

steering wheel. I'm also now limping from the painful dog nip, head still thumps, eye throbbing.

Now I've lived in Jacksdale all my life and still get the names of the terraced streets mixed up. Another No.53 on another street proves to be the wrong one. Eventually after calling back home to find Malc's contact details I head in the right direction.

As I go up Laverick Road I see this little, broad fellow, with a fifties hairstyle, standing outside his house checking his watch like he's back on Topper door duty and I'm a punter hurrying to get in before the last orders and late night lock in. I know this is him.

I get out of the car and walk towards him –

'Malc?'

'Yeah, bloody hell, yuh look like you've done ten rounds with Mike Tyson or had a night in the Topper he, he. Come on in.'

I stop to stroke his dog, which is a westy like our 'Whisky dog.' His is 14 and has a poorly eye. Malc's missus asks if I'd like a bitter lemon and Malc shows me into the welcomingly cool front room. An envelope stuffed with old promotional band photographs lies on the settee, next to a big folder that contains Topper photos along side other old Jacksdale pictures; The pit, old railway station, viaduct, floods and a great photo of Malc sat on Jacksdale motorbike ace John Newbold's Suzuki racing bike.

I ask Malc about the early days.

Malc: Alf lived in a caravan behind the building with Emma and the kids whilst the renovation took place. At first, being a club, it had to have a membership for its customers. This caused problems when people from outside the area came to see an act. Membership cards were passed out of the toilet window, some nights the same person came in five times before I clicked on.

Alf and his partners realised then that there wasn't actually a pub as such in the village (only a welfare, social club and the Portland but that was still known as a hotel) so applied for a licence to make the Grey Topper a pub and do away from a restricting licence.

Eventually the effort paid off, in March 1969 English cricketing legend Fred Trueman and chart toppers The Searchers were the guests of honour at the opening night of the Grey Topper as a live music venue.

They asked me to be the doorman. Jo and George Wakeman did the cellar and garden.

His dog nudges it's way into the front room and comes to me for some fuss.

'Gerr aht on it,' says Malc.

'He's alright I love dogs,' (except Jack Russells I think feeling the throb in my foot).

Malc: They had one at Topper yuh know?

I have been told about this...

Spike: They had a huge dog, it used to be kept in this shed, which would rock from side to side from the dog moving about inside and going mental trying to get out. One day it escaped and got onto the stage with the strippers.

Malc: Yeah that's the one. Lance it wer called, a Bullmastiff, it wer seventeen stone.

'Wow! The weight of heavy weight boxer.'

Malc: Yeah, one night, someone had left a chip carton in the middle of the road. Lance had got out and smelling a fish supper went to fetch this carton. The C5 hit him

'C5?'

'Yeah double decker bus from Alfreton.'

'Ah.'

'Bus had a mighty dint in it.'

'It would.'

'We had to put Lance on a pallet, five on us, to take him to the vet's. He survived for a while but died shortly after.'

'Poor Lance.' (bet strippers were relieved though).

'Rene played piano, Wednesday and Friday, old uns came along for a sing-a-long. We had Bingo nights of course but with winning lines of £75, £85 and £90, that was a lot of money then. There was old time dancing on Monday's, Saturday morning discos for kids. So yuh see Alf wasn't just catering for young uns and rock music. It was an entertainment palace for the whole village.'

You can't please all the people all the time?

Malc: No there was some moaning gits, the sort of people who never go out and socialise, just sit in watching the television. The sort that complain to the council just for something to do. Alf always had obstacles thrown in front of him by the council, magistrates and police. He'd despair at times.

A woman from the council came down to inspect the plans for the proposed Topper extension. She wasn't happy with the plans, how certain parts of the building were laid out in relation to the street, fire exits and so on.

Alf walked over, took the plans out of her hands and turned them around. 'You've got them upside down,' he pointed out.

She gets on her high horse then and focuses on the beer tanks, too many too big, unhygienic etc –

'What if I have those removed?' She warned.

'Well him (Malc) and me will have the time of our lives drinking them dry now.' Alf replied.

One time, when he was having trouble getting a late licence, there was this vicar Father Francis, a bit like one out of *Father*

Ted, he owned a pub, he acted as a character witness for Alf. For his help he was asked what he wanted as a thank you, he pointed to the till. 'Oh the takings for the night will be fine.'

He was intelligent was Alf and well liked by the bands he booked. People like Brian Connolly of The Sweet and Les Gray from Mud would turn up hours early on Sundays to chat and listen to Alf and get fed, they said it was the only place they could get a decent meal on the road. One time Screaming Lord Sutch lost his car keys and had to wait hours for the AA, but he wasn't bothered as he was enjoying himself so much.

Alf did a lot for charity, raising money for guide dogs for the blind. He sent Brutby hospital - were he was treated when ill – a hamper and champagne and paid for a stain glass window there. There was another hospital that was struggling with heating bills, Alf used to send them bags of coal.

I ask how he feels to see the Topper being demolished.

Malc: Sad, first the Portland was pulled down, now the Topper, there'll be no entertainment and life left in the village soon. I'm wondering if they'll find the time capsule.

Time capsule?

'Yeah when we changed the location of the stage we put all this memorabilia in a time capsule and buried it under the stage.

I tell Malc that at least he's got fantastic memories of the place and was lucky to be around at the time and be so involved.

'I've got something else, hold on,' He says going over to a cupboard. 'When it closed they asked me to take anything I wanted. All I did want was this.'

He puts a little Scottish and Newcastle statuette on the mantle piece –

'Worth a bob a two nah, but to me it tells me stories of the Topper.'

I'm wondering about the right time to bring up the subject of the fire when...Malc leans forward, mischievous glint in his eye.

Malc: Of course it came to an end with the fire, got to be careful what I say, don't want to say owt incriminating but it was a bit.....

BABYLON'S BURNING 3

'Last week I wrote about the disgraceful mess left by a rock festival in Stevenage that I had the misfortune to witness as I drove by. "The desecration I cannot describe. And the people - unwashed, unshaven, wandering down the verge like Gypsies. I had to swerve several times as they staggered into the middle of the road dazed and confused.

I would never want to see permission to allow such groups in Ashfield, because I for one would not like Ashfield to be left like some vast council rubbish dump it would take an age to clean after they had gone their dirty ways"

The item brought the following response, which I reproduce in all its glory, spelling errors and all. Unfortunately this pop fan did not have the courage to sign his/her name. However after reading it, I'm no longer wondering why the festival was a bomb site after a few silly groups played to their devotees.'

'Dear Sillybag Bennett

I was one of the people fortunate enough to get a ticket to see Led Zeppelin at Knebworth. I seen the worst of the rubbish left and a regiment of soldiers could have cleared it in a day. You said the people were scruffy. I suppose you would be clean and tidy after camping rough for a few nights, then sitting in a field for sixteen hours waiting for the immortal Led Zeppelin.

You also referred to us as children. There was not one person who was not mentally more adult than you. About having rock concerts in Ashfield. No self respecting rock band would gob on it. What is Ashfield anyway if not a rubbish dump.

Yours – Spirit of Woodstock

Ps You remind me of my gran and she's been dead ten years.

Pps – At least litter can be cleared up not like the destruction left by football thugs, so why not ban football?'

Well-said 'Spirit of Woodstock,' but rock acts were on in Ashfield and at the Grey Topper the punters gobbed on them, not the other way around, and there were football thugs to boot, or should that be football thugs booting people?

In the news -

Concerns from the public about 'anti social spray paint slogans and other graffiti and damage to telephone kiosks.'

'When I were a lad even the village idiot would ring the police if something was amiss.' A local Chief Inspector comments.

Five bra's and ten pairs of pants worth £25 stolen from Nuncagate.

A gang of 'incredible Hulks' are ripping off garage doors and stealing cars in Kikby.

Me and my mates were finding more diverse things to fill the longs days of the summer holidays. We tried the jokes, games and ideas given to us by kids programme *Why Don't You*, like trying to make a hovercraft out of matchbox's, tissue paper and your mums and sisters hair dryer. It blew up so we switched off our TV's and did something less boring instead.

With mum, dad and brother at work and sister staying with friends. We had the run of the house to our selves. I'd lost in the final of the Subbuteo World Cup.

The butt of our next joke was this poor little westy dog that we were looking after for a neighbouring family while they were on holiday. Its name was Sid and a normally timid thing.

'Let's mek Sid Vicious,' I suggested.

96

With punk music blaring out in the background we put safety pins in his tartan coat, sellotaped on shades and spiked up his hair with mum's Harmony hairspray, dying it green with food colouring.

We were in hysterics at this site, when the front door opened, and dad limped into view. A forklift truck had ran over his foot at work and he'd been sent to the hospital then home early.

'What the bloody…' He started then 'Aaaarrrgghhh.' As Sid made a bolt for it, viciously savaging dad's bandage foot as he went, before pogoing over the gate to freedom. My record collection came to a halt that month, I'd no pocket money to spend.

*

In keeping with the Led Zeppelin, Knebworth gig it was a bit of a heavy metal month at the Topper. I didn't like 'grebs' at the time (especially after one stole my girlfriend). They still wore flares, stunk, and at school discos they looked stupid all stood in a circle, legs apart, hands on hips, bopping their long haired heads like they were throwing up over the side of a sinking boat and swinging their arms up and down like they were scooping out the water. Mum agreed after we passed a greb - about my age - in the street one day.

'Sometimes I'm glad you're a punk, I don't have to try too hard with your clothes do I. Not like their mums, all them patches covering their jackets, it must be "oh mum can you sew this patch on, oh mum can you sew this patch on, oh mum"….and smelly petunia oil, if you accidentally mixed that up with a bunch of clothes, that's your whole wash ruined.'

The Topper was known as a greb hangout before punk took over. UFO had played there and many NWOBHM (New Wave Of British Heavy Metal) bands including Judas Priest. Girlschool showed up in 1978, but at least they were clued up enough to mix punk and metal like Motorhead (and years before Nirvana.)

Kelly Johnson - Girlschool: Mixing punk and metal, we definitely had that cross-over thing going at the time - although not particularly intentionally, it was all just part of that whole 'just get up there and thrash-it-out' thing at the time ... and I do remember one of our first gigs at that time was playing support to Sham 69 at the Harlesden Roxy in London in front of a few hundred hard-core punks and not getting gobbed on - dunno if that was a good thing or not really!

Saxon were on at the Topper in August with songs about motorcycles and street fighting. Their biggest hit 'Wheels Of Steel' would hit the charts 7 months later. Other NWOBHM bands on that month were Chrome Molly, Race Against Time and Ritz. Still, the Topper punks still held sway.

Mick Clark: I remember letting Marsy have one of my Sed's stringy mohair's for a gig and a fuckin ugly hairy greb, who was old enough to know better, ripped it for a laugh. He and his mates had come along to a punk gig just to take the piss. Within a second of him ripping my jumper, Marsy and our mates from Derby hammered the cunt and all his mates fucked off. Who's laughing now boys and close the door on your way out, welcome to the Grey Topper circa 1979. 'I don't care about long hair - I don't wear flares!'

I was upstairs with my brother Brian and his punk rock electric guitar.

After several frustrating months of neither of us even being capable at putting three chords of acceptable discordant noise together, we settle for the smashing of a guitar image of rock 'n' roll.

One of the few things I ever did manage to learn to play on a guitar, before deciding I wasn't going to be a rock star, was the intro to 'Warhead' by the UK Subs.

In the summer of 79 I bought their single 'Stranglehold' in

98

blood red vinyl. I held this up to my eyes and watched the world turn Day-Glo

In the Topper a local sailor stood in amazement and watched the world turn pogo. Having been away travelling the seven seas, punk had by and large passed him by.

'Fuckin ell. I've been in the navy nine years and travelled all over the world, but never experienced a vibe like this,' Brek said turning to Steve Singleton.

They were stood at the back of the room, looking over a mass of bouncing head's, their owners whipped up into a frenzy by the 3-minute powers chords of the UK Subs. Then they blew the amps.

Charlie Harper - UK Subs: I remember using our Marshall stacks as a P.A. The Topper crowd didn't mind at all when they blew, yes a good lot they were.

Mick Clark: Charlie Harper of the subs was also fantastic and always willing to chat. I remember taking him and I think Pete Davies down to the Chinese takeaway for something to eat - they wouldn't go to the chippy over the road, its reputation had even reached fuckin London!

Nicky Garratt - UK Subs: I do remember playing the Grey Topper indeed. It was a semi regular stop for us.

Pete Davies – UK Subs: One thing I remember was the gobbing at the Grey Topper was extreme, there was so much on the guitars that I remember Paul taking his hand off the neck and a ribbon of gob from his hand still attached to the bass...and stalactites (gobicles) hanging from the beam above the stage. My old Slingerland drum kit still bears the scars.

UK Subs were one of the best of the second-generation punk bands, that summer saw them reaching their peak. *Sounds* music paper had just made 'Stranglehold' joint single of the week (with The Ruts 'Babylon's Burning'). It would sell 75,000 copies and give them their first *Top of the Pops* appearance. The director of the Sex Pistols *The Great Rock 'n' Roll Swindle* Julien Temple had made a film about them called *Punk Can Take It*. This was shown as a support to the notorious film *Scum* that depicted borstal life and starred a young Ray Winstone.

Nicky Garratt: It was a great time for me, but different. Into the mix you have to add business, travel, fame, (some) money, work (song-writing) – so for me it was a multi dimensional time. Things happened fast and big, *Top Of The Pops*, huge shows and meeting very famous people. When we made *Another Kind of Blues* we used Ian Gillian's studio. Deep Purple were like gods to us in the early 1970's, and there I was in my full punk gear drinking in a pub with him.

One person who wasn't impressed by the vibe of the UK Subs was Topper owner Alf.

Tink: The Subs had raided the small bar and nicked a load of beer. Alf was going nuts, saying 'right that's it they're barred.'

Charlie Harper: I'm afraid nothings changed. If we've had a good show at a venue we all stay in the bar telling ourselves how great we were and get blotto.

Pete Davies: I remember sitting quietly in the van waiting to leave when a there was a knock on the window beside me, on opening it a roadie (RC2) handed me bottles of Creme de menth and whiskey, 'quick Pete stash these.' Then everyone piling into the van with suspicious clunking from bags and making a hasty exit , party on.........

Mick Clark: We followed them around for a while and saw them play at Leicester, Nottingham, Derby, Sheffield and Retford on more than one occasion. Charlie Harper once said 'Hello Jacksdale,' before a gig in Leicester because he recognised us.

Little known group The Injectors were on the bill one Sunday a few weeks later. But New Wave nights were spiralling out of control, the Topper had not only become a mecca for punks in the area, it was also becoming the venue for gangs from miles around to meet and settle their differences.

Spike: I don't know if it was The Injectors gig, but it had all kicked off. I was walking this girl home to Selston, but every road we went down was blocked by police. In the end I had to cut through the pit yard and go over the fields. That didn't turn out a bad option though he, he.

I'd been out with my parents, we'd had a nice walk through the countryside to the village of Riddings and spent the night at a pub there. As we walked back at the end of the night and approached Jacksdale a gang of youths were brawling in the street. One had the other pinned down in the middle of the road, a knife to his throat. Mam had to drag my dad away so he didn't get involved.

Around the corner on the road that rang along side the Topper were half a dozen police vehicles – two Black Maria's and four cars – waiting for the main event, closing time at the Topper.

We lived on the very edge of Jacksdale, about half a mile away, up a steep hill, through a council estate and one of the last houses before you go into Westwood. Yet on the back garden - and in the bedroom with the window open - you could hear it after the Topper doors burst open and it spilled out onto the street – shouts, screams, sirens and breaking glass.

Ballroom Blitz

The industrial Midlands 1972-1975, miners on strike, the 3 day week, overtime bans and power cuts.

Alf decided to get around this by buying a generator from a farm at Crich. Unfortunately this made any organ in a band sound a bit discordant.

Ally: It played E flat instead of C sharp or something like that, it made this farting noise anyway. It nearly caused the break up of several bands as they'd turn around angrily to the organ player and blame them for messing up the sound.

One night Raymond Froggatt was on. They asked him if he wanted to play one long set or split his act into two 45-minute halves. He chose the latter, but when he picked up the guitar he only managed one strum before the power went.

Time to put our new generator into action, but when we went to turn it on the battery was flat.

Undaunted Raymond Froggatt told them to clear the tables and chairs to one side, for everyone to sit on the floor, candles were lit, jugs of ale filled and he took out his acoustic guitar and did an unplugged set years before MTV made it a popular departure for bands like Nirvana.

After an hour he said 'I'd play longer but it looks like the Newcastle Brown Ale has run out.'

At that moment pints of it appeared before him and he played on.

These were the 'winters of discontent,' but at least the residents of Jacksdale could step out of reality and into Alf's dream palace at the weekend, dance and drink (and f**k no doubt) the night away and be entertained by some of the biggest music names around. For the years 1972-75 were the Grey Topper's heydays.

Topper Life On Mars 1973 - 'Wahrrdy' looks on as Ralph Amott attempts to take his yard old ale crown or top hat perhaps. 'Wahrrdy' apparently used to have a light on his hat that lit up to signal he wanted serving whilst at the bar, was barred from one pub for eating a live mouse, was the person to ask for the time as he had an alarm clock attached to a chain inside his coat and once broke his legs jumping through a pub window.

I'm astonished at the names on the clubs records that Ally has given me. Soul greats The Drifters, Ben E King, Chaka Khan, Edwin Starr, Geno Washington!

Mick Twomey (Nottstalgia.com): I saw Edwin Starr for the first time at the Grey Topper. What a fantastic night. He stood back to leave the whole audience singing 'SOS'. I've been a tremendous fan of the man ever since that night.

Within years the name Grey Topper had spread far beyond the surrounding pit villages. Youths from inner city Nottingham were forsaking the clubs on their doorstep and undertaking the arduous quest of finding Jacksdale.

I get a call from a guy who lived in Clifton, a suburb of Nottingham.

'We first heard about the Grey Topper on Radio Trent when

they did live shows from there. We were into Northern Soul so thought we'd check the place out. A group of us piled into car and set off.

I was driving, my mate navigating at the side of me, he took out this road map, studied it for a while and said "Jacksdale's not on here, where is it?" We were driving around for hours, we stopped to ask people directions but no one had heard of Jacksdale. Then you'd mention the Grey Topper. "Oh yeah I've heard of that." But they couldn't tell you were it was.

Eventually we came across this road sign in the middle of nowhere with it on, it pointed down a steep hill, descending down into fog, into the valley. We had some great nights down there, as soon as we did know were it was. I remember this great Northern Soul dancer called "Rubber Legs Roy" with white bleached hair.'

It was like a magic spell had fallen on the village, where teenagers could turn on *Top Of The Pops* and climb inside their TV's and be there. Especially when the Take That of their day - The Bay City Rollers showed up on the 'what's on' posters outside the Topper. On this occasion, though, the plug was nearly pulled, breaking transmission and a few hundred teenage girls hearts.

Ally Key: The lads came in looking pleased with themselves, tartan in place, then looked around and said 'Where's our road crew?' We looked at each other nonplussed 'you tells us?'

After a few frantic phone calls they announced that their gear had been impounded on a ferry in Jersey. There was only a few hours before they went on. We dipped deep in our pockets, then I drove like a madman down to this place in Mansfield that sold instruments and hired some from there. Couldn't find a mandolin for love nor money though. No one noticed how poor their sound was thanks to girls screaming.

Malc Fletcher: Groupies were always trying to get in the dressing room to be with the pop stars. There was a fire door at the back, it had light above it that came on when the door was opened, so when we saw this we knew the groupies had been let in.

There was this time, I reckon it was one of the Bay City Rollers, he'd gone missing and his band mates were impatient to get going and sent me looking for him. I found him shagging this groupie around the back of the Topper. He told me to tell them to give him 5 minutes as he'd decided to give an encore.

It was glam rock, of course, that was the most popular music of the time. Blackfoot Sue from Birmingham played the Topper so many times that their Top 40 hits 'Standing In The Road' and 'Sing Don't Speak' became village anthems. Brian Johnson – later of AC/DC fame - took to the stage with his glam band Geordie. Alvin Stardust coo-ca-choo'd. And Gary Glittered long before his fall from a height even greater than those of his platform sole boots.

Ally: The first time Gary Glitter was booked they got lost in the fog and couldn't find the place, at least women could unlock their daughters.

Tony Oglesby: I think it must have been the Glitter Band's first tour. They'd just had 'Angel Face' in the charts but clearly lacked much other material. They came on stage to a fairly warm welcome but by the third rendition of 'Angel Face' the crowd had turned on them. 'This is the worse place we've played,' the lead singer announced whilst ducking to avoid empty plastic glasses as they rained in on stage. The booing continued and they all quickly left the stage.

The favourites were - glam personified - The Sweet. I can remember the buzz around the village the night The Sweet were due to appear shortly after 'Blockbuster' had been No.1 in the charts (their fourth and final gig at the Grey Topper). My brother was mad on them, had all their records and had put a huge poster of them on the wall of the bedroom we shared.

I liked their music, in fact they were the first group I was into, but my child's mind was totally confused to what sex they were. So I asked my brother and sister.

'They're androgynous,' they told me.

'What are they?'

'It's a species from another planet.'

'What, they like came down in spaceships to Jacksdale to play us music?'

'Yeah.'

I looked back up at the poster and believed it.

Dad was just as confused but was never going to buy the alien species story.

'What the bloody hell? Aye they got silver handbags n'all? Glam, huh. I'll tell yuh what, forget Pan's People, they're bloody Pansy people. That's what. And our Tony here, what's a picture like that doing to his mind. Birds and bees ah can explain to him, but that lot, bloody hell.'

Steve Priest - The Sweet: My parents were horrified too when I first went on in glam. We never actually saw ourselves as glam, we considered ourselves a heavy rock band. But we wore all this glam and glitter because of *Top Of The Pops*, everyone was trying to out do each other, it got a bit silly, a bit Monty Python.

Andy Scott – The Sweet: We went glam after seeing Marc Bolan and the success he was having. When we first played the Grey Topper we weren't glam, though, that came later, we were a touring band playing a variety of music, a lot of covers. We'd do 2 sets of 45 minutes, doing medleys of mainly The Who songs, but liked to mix it up like throwing in Motown songs, alongside heavier material like Black Sabbaths 'Paranoid' and Led

Zeppelin's 'Whole Lotta Love'. Blues songs like Jimmy Read's 'You Got Me Runnin'.' Brian (Connolly, Sweet's magnetic lead singer) had a great versatile voice, he was magical on songs like 'Great Balls of Fire.'

Steve Priest: Ye Gods the Grey Topper! I remember playing it well. In the early days it was one of the many gigs we did to stay solvent or close thereto. They were a good crowd and got better each time we played. The girls were nice especially if you stayed overnight in a rather cheap hotel!

Never mind the Sweet bollox: The glam kings show punk attitude way before the Sex Pistols and their followers were causing outrage for displaying the same messages and imagery on their clothes.

Andy Scott: In the span of our gigs at the Grey Topper we went from being mainly a covers band, staying at cheap hotels, driving ourselves with no real roadie to help carry in our PA in 1971. To being number one in the charts on *Top of the Pops* - with a whole road crew transporting three to five tonnes of gear - and running from masses of screaming girl fans to get into a limo to be driven home after gigs in 1973.

Sweet were on their way to selling over 50 million records worldwide. But their last 'Blockbuster' gig at the Grey Topper caught them at their glam rock peak. Just a year later – in 1974 – the sad decline of lead singer Brian Connolly had begun. His drinking was already a noticeable problem to the rest of the band (even though they were no shirkers of indulging in the full on sex, drugs and rock 'n' roll lifestyle themselves), but then a savage attack outside a nightclub would speed up his fall as the charismatic frontman of one of the most popular bands of the decade.

Andy Scott: Today he wouldn't have been alone that night, but you thought you were invincible then. It was during the recording sessions for the *Sweet Fanny Adams* album. Brian had gone into this West London club and some guys didn't like the attention he was getting from some girls. They followed him outside and started jumping all over his Mercedes, when he challenged them they beat him up, one of them kicked him in his throat. His vocal chords were left badly damaged.

Now I've heard a lot of conspiracy theories about this, like that's what they set out to do, that it was a set up, but why would they do that? I asked Brian about this and he said he didn't really remember anything. He wasn't able to sing again for some time after that, but his voice never fully recovered. It left him mentally scarred too and his excessive drinking and smoking didn't help, it all took its toll on his voice and on his health in general.

Brian Connolly did sing on the Sweet hits 'Fox On The Run' (1975) and 'Love Is Like Oxygen' (1978 – that earned Andy Scott a Ivor Novello nomination) but his alcoholism and erratic behaviour had all but isolated him from the rest of the band. During the recording of the album *Level Headed* - at Clearwell Castle - Connolly was anything but level headed, jumping from a 50ft high window for a bet and firing a shotgun over the cowering heads of his band mates into a bird sanctuary.

The final straw came on Sweet's 1978 tour of the U.S.A. Connolly was so drunk on stage – in front of studio bosses - that he had to be dragged off after a few numbers. He parted company with Sweet in 1979. The rest of the band split themselves in 1981, several splinter groups were formed and there was a very brief reunion of the classic line-up, but it came to nothing. Brian Connolly died of alcohol related liver failure and a heart attack in 1997 aged 51.

Andy Scott: I like to remember the Grey Topper era Sweet - good days, happy days, innocent days!

*

So Alf had built it and they had come. Those dreams he'd had, when living in the caravan, trying to turn a crumbling old cinema into a top music venue had been fulfilled.

There were however many a *Spinal Tap*-esque bands on the circuit. One such was Light Fantastic.

Steve Priest - The Sweet: Every time we played the Topper this guy came up and said 'Have yuh fookin seen Light Fantastic yet?' Then one night they supported us there. Which was an eye opener.

Phil Hodgkinson: They used to issue a warning before they came on stage 'Anyone with a nervous disposition don't watch us.' They had all these strobe lights and this singer pretended to saw into his arm, all this green blood spurting everywhere, then they hung a woman on stage. Right ham Hammer Horror.

Marsy: Yeah and this dry ice smoke swirling about and a coffin at the front of the stage that this local chap, who used to follow them about, always came out of.

To Alf this could have represented the demons that threatened to turn his dream into a nightmare. He had a great music venue, but you can't have a club with the beer flowing until 2.00 am without the inevitable trouble that comes with it.

Spike: It was like the Wild West at times, they actually had saloon doors - after the main doors - that people passed through into the club, or came flying out through when it kicked off, and then either roll their sleeves up and go and get stuck back in or land knocked out on the foyer floor, then the doormen would dump them outside.

Some people did their best to avoid a fight by taking their anger out on objects instead of people.

Tig Langton: The toilet looked like an aquarium, all these green tiles and a glass fish tank water cistern. I punched that one night - when I was mad about something - it shattered and covered all these youths in water that were stood having a piss. Nearly caused a bigger fight than one I was trying to avoid.

As a kid I was aware of Jacksdale's rough reputation to outsiders, but if you were a resident it was a great place to live, great community spirit. My childhood was brilliant growing up there, I had loads of friends, rarely had any trouble from anyone, and bullies were put in their place by the real tough lads who knew how to fight but didn't need prove it, unless pushed or the gauntlet was thrown down. If outsiders came to the Topper looking for trouble, then they'd find it. There was many a *Saturday Night Sunday Morning*, Arthur Seaton type - 'I'm not barmy, I'm a fighting pit prop that wants a pint of beer.'

If you want to know how far afield the Grey Topper's reputation spread, consider this. When doing a Google search, I came across a mention of it in a Middlesbrough forum. They were discussing another club that had a bad image and someone responds with – 'What as tough as the Grey Topper, Jacksdale?'

If even people from Middlesbrough are using the Grey Topper as a benchmark for how tough something is, then that says it all!

BABYLON'S BURNING 2

13,14 It's a teenage warning
15, 16 But nobody's listening
17, 18 Who takes the blame
19, 20 The twentieth century
'Teenage Warning' – Angelic Upstarts

September 1979

In the news –

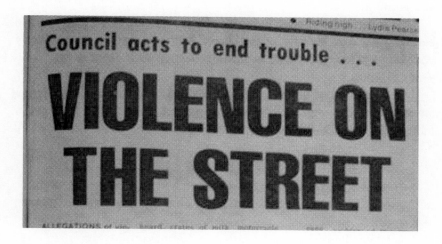

Allegations of violence spilling into the street after punk concerts at an Ashfield nightclub, have forced a parish council into action.

Selston Parish Council are to demand the removal of the entertainment licence for the Grey Topper Club at Jacksdale…and angry residents want the liquor licence revoked as well.

The decision for strong action came on Tuesday after the Parish Council had heard a series of allegations about the behaviour of 'fans' attending the club.

The members were told at the meeting that punk rock bands had allegedly encouraged their audience to spit at each other and drench each other in beer.

TROUBLE

And, it was claimed, this was the start of trouble, which spilled into the street at closing time, terrifying residents in the early hours of the morning.

Councillor Ken Clarke said one teenager had described fans bizarre antics, which included buying beer to pour over each other.

And the council heard, crates of milk bottles had been thrown through bus windows and nearby homes, many belonging to the elderly, had been besieged by gangs of youths and motorcyclists.

A petition of more than 150 signatures from incensed residents, who describe the late night action as 'terrorism', is to be sent to licensing justices in an attempt to prevent owner Mr Alfred Hyslop from getting his liquor licence renewed.

And in a letter to Nottinghamshire Chief Constable Charles McLachlan, MP Frank Haynes pointed out that trouble starts with late night battles between rival gangs of youths who use bottles as ammunition.

"It is futile for anyone living nearby the Selston Road club to go to bed before 2 a.m. because of the chaos. And even earlier, some elderly residents are too frightened to venture outside their front doors," said Frank Haynes.

One resident of Main Road, Jacksdale, told the council that during an early morning outbreak he had to get out of bed after he heard a motorcycle gang besieging a house nearby.

PROBLEM

"I knew the woman's husband was on a night shift so she might be in trouble. The youths finally went away after one hour and the woman was terrified,' he said.

Selston Chairman, Coun. Arthur Skevington, said "terrorism" was not too strong a word to describe the incidents.

He said that although it was a police matter, it would need an army of constables to tackle a problem of this magnitude.

A club member of staff told the council he was aware of the trouble and had even tried to control it himself but as it was outside the premises he felt it was a matter for the police.

Club licensee, Mr. Hyslop told the meeting the motorcycle gangs were nothing to do with his club. He added that in more than three years he had been in trouble on only one occasion and this involved a fight between grown men and not youths.

GILLIAN BENNETT as I see it...

A group of little punk urchins were waiting in the rain for our club to open, this a yowf club, around the road from the Topper, in an extension behind a chapel. The place hadn't had any money spent on it for years and looked how it would in the early 1970's except in a more dilapidated state.

The table football pitch had a bigger slope than Yeovil's due to a broken leg, and the blue teams entire defence was missing (fortunately though they faced down hill so this sort of balanced things up a bit.) The table tennis table didn't have any legs at all. Floor tennis would be the apt name, you had to learn to dance like a Russian Cossack to be able to have a game. The cloth of the rickety, tiny old pool table had more rips in it than Johnny Rotten's jumper.

There were so many holes around the dartboard that just a few more wayward arrows would cause the board to fall to the ground leaving a porthole in its place. The game mousetrap didn't even have a mouse, it having escaped years before and scurried into one of the many holes in the skirting board. Scrabble had hardly any vowels so we couldn't amuse ourselves with blue Scrabble putting double word scores like 'knackers,' 'fuck,' 'twat' and 'wanker.'

Paint peeled from the walls (it would be another eight years before it had a fresh lick of paint. I should know, as it was me that applied it when working as a decorator for the council.)

Worst of all was the record collection – The Osmonds, Jacksons, Cassidy's, Carpenters, Worzels. These to be played on a knackered old player the stylus of which hadn't been changed since Hendrix took to the stage at Woodstock.

Was this the best the village had to keep the kids off the streets and entertained? Well we'd had enough, tonight we were taking it and we'd brought our own records along.

The long suffering chap who ran the place – with a bible bashing lady – always turned up late with the keys to let us in, especially on rainy nights.

But we didn't care, the later the better. Eddie Bradley had discovered that a window could be prised open. He was in there now and soon emerged with a bottles of sherry, whisky and Jesus blood from the cupboard in the office, along with chocolate bars and sweets that were supposed to be sold to us later. We all took a swig, then Eddie squeezed his way back in, to top the bottles up with water before putting them back where he found them.

When he let us in, the man who ran the yowf club, was surprised to find us in such high spirits, but a little dismayed when none of us went to buy anything from the sweet cupboard. Then agitated with the raucous racket reverberating around the club.

We put all our favourites on, the sounds and songs we could identify with - The Members, The Stranglers, UK Subs, The Clash, Angelic Upstarts, The Dammed, The Skids - 'Into the Valley' had almost become Jacksdale's theme tune, with armies of youths marching down the hills into the village ready to do battle. We loved the b-side 'T V Stars.'

'ALBERT TATLOCK – ALBERT TATLOCK,' we chanted.

Then, best of all, the Sex Pistols, still the group guaranteed to cause offence to our elders. None more so than 'Friggin In The Riggin'

'It was on the good ship Venus
By Christ ya shoulda seen us
The figurehead was a whore in bed
And the mast, a mammoth penis
Friggin in the riggin
Friggin in the riggin
Friggin in the riggin
There was fuck all else to do.'

We joyously sang pogoing about the room. The man – after giving his colleague some smelling salts and a bible – pulled the plug.

A riot ensued, the crap old early 70's records were used as missiles. I've got to admit hurling 'Crazy Horses' by The Osmonds against a wall and seeing it shatter into pieces was one of the most satisfying moments of my young life.

We piled out onto the waste ground at the side of the club. A row of old terraced houses were due for demolition, we vented our frustration on those, chucking bricks through the windows, one lad sprayed Day-Glo graffiti on the walls.

Then we realised we'd be cordoned in, our exit blocked, the village police had arrived. Which in this case was the elderly flat-capped pigeon-fancying brigade. They'd been over the road in the function room of a local pub, displaying their feathered friends. With baskets on pram wheels joined up to form an impenetrable barrier they closed in on us.

'Oh fuck, the cappers, the cooler,' shouted one panic stricken mate.

He'd done time in the cooler before, when we dared him to knock on a cappers door and ask for the wrong time.

'Wrong time, wrong time, Is'll bloody gi thee wrong time.' The capper Adolphus Tims (I kid you not) had grabbed and thrown him into the coal shed, locked the door and left him there for a few hours.

'Nah then yuh little bogger what's the wrong time?' He was

asked on his release, followed by a kick up the backside.

We managed to kick in an old back gate of one of the empty houses and escape up the backs.

Around the road at the Topper later that night, The Angelic Upstarts were ripping through their set. 'I'm An Upstart', 'Teenage Warning.'

The crowd were energised, but not pogoing en mass, divisions split the bodies into groups.

Singo: You could cut the atmosphere with a knife.

Feff: Someone did.

By the time the Angelic Upstarts arrived at the Topper they'd already had two Top 40 hits (the two singles mentioned above), which is more success than Adam and the Ants or Simple Minds had had at the time. So were guaranteed to sell out the place.

Mensi – Angelic Upstarts: I remember the place, middle of nowhere but a good-sized venue. I was drinking in a bar 2 minutes walk from the club and I remember getting told to go on stage, so I wandered over and the doorman asked for me ticket –

'I'm the singer in the Angelics,' I told him.

'Yes mate I've heard that one a 100 times before.'

'But look, that's me picture on the poster.'

'Don't look like you,' he says.

'Ok mate I'm going back to the pub over there, when they start looking for me that's where I'll be, but you have to come get me ok?'

'Don't hold your breath waiting for me coming,' he says.

'I wont.'

Ten minutes later he shows up all red in the face. I looked at him and we both just burst out laughing.

Singer Tommy 'Mensi' Mensforth and guitarist Ray Cowie, known as Mond were disaffected youths from a northeast council estate when they formed the Upstarts in the summer of 77.

Mensi – Angelic Upstarts: We started in a youth club in 1977. I got into punk after hearing 'Boredom' by the Buzzcocks and seeing The Clash's power and energy on the 'White Riot' tour. I wanted it, the lot.

With an angry punk sound and volatile anti-establishment, anit-facist and anti-racist lyrics, violence often erupted at their gigs.

Mensi – Angelic Upstarts: In them days you went to a fight and an Upstarts gig broke out. The only fight I would remember is if we were involved ourselves, which was frequently.

They once did a gig in a prison and nearly kicked off a riot when the cons turned up to see a union jack embellished with the words 'Upstarts Army', a clenched fist and the motto 'Smash Law And Order' with a pig in a police helmet entitled 'PC Fuck Pig'.

Often they would smash up a real pigs head on stage. First single 'Murder of Liddle Towers' (about police brutality) caught the attention of Sham 69's Jimmy Pursey who produced their debut album *Teenage Warning*.

Singo: You just knew it was going to blow up as the gig was coming to an end, I was out of there and around to the welfare.

The atmosphere of a punk gig and the Angelic Upstarts edgy lyrics may have poured fuel onto the flickering flames, but according to one local the trouble that flared up was football related and none of those who started it were from Jacksdale.

Phil Hodgkinson: They were gangs of Forest fans from Sutton and Eastwood with a score to settle. Some lad had taken a beating at a match and one side blamed the other for not backing them up.

On the terraces supporting the same team they'd be united, now from separate towns it was back to territorial pissings. Whatever the reason, at the gigs end it kicked off. Like one of the regular floods to hit Jacksdale, it burst out onto the street with the force of a tsunami.

Fists flew, doc martens swung in running battles, then they loaded up with weapons. Fence posts were ripped up and milkman Ally Key's bottles were far too readily available stored in crates at the side of the Topper.

Tink: It was like the English Civil War. One gang was on one side of the street, pulling bottles out of crates and sending a volley over into the middle of the other gang. Then they'd retaliate by charging, wielding fence posts, giving out a war cry.

Spike: There was this youth, Alan somebody, a right poseur and big-headed twat anyway. He pulled up at the junction in his brand new green Vauxhall Viva, then turned green himself as his car was surrounded and its windows were smashed in.

Phil Hodgkinson: Henny was on top of the bus shelter with the Pye Hill No.2 sign (Pye Hill was the name of Jacksdale's pit). 'What you doin up there?' I asked.

'If any come near me they'll get this round there fuckin head,' he replied.

One lad fell over the fence and into the stream by the Portland. Some youth came over ready to lay into me, but others recognised me from Forest so let me off.

Feff: There was glass everywhere, strewn all over the road as far as the chemists (about 300 yards away). When the Angelic Upstarts left the Topper in their van you should have seen the look on their faces at the chaos around them.

If you lived in Jacksdale at least you could get away from the trouble in the refuge of your home. Or perhaps not?

Tink: I'd gone home and went to bed, this was ages after the gig ended and we lived hundreds of yards away from the Topper at the end of Laverick Road. Then my mum burst into my bedroom with a poker. I asked her what was up and she said there was all these youths battling in our garden. I went out in my pyjamas wielding this poker but these youths were punks, so sort of mates.

They ran for it went the police came up the street. They'd blocked the road, there was all these youths running off down gardens over the backs and across the fields to escape, the trouble, the village and the police.

Sally Renshaw: The fighting was really scary, there was chaos and destruction everywhere including in the outlying fields. I was petrified, some chic London girls started to pick on me and

and my mate Alison, much older than us too - good job we knew the area and ran off down the Red Road shitting ourselves, we got rescued by a lad called Nipper on his motorbike!

Incensed residents woke the following morning to a scene of devastation, more Topper tales of terror and several sons with busted noses and black eyes. And now many banded together determined to get the club shut down.

Alf had before him the biggest fight so far to keep the Grey Topper open.

In Rainbows

By the mid 1970's Alf was in a constant battle to keep the Topper dream alive. There seems to be a report every other month in the local press about his court appearances.

Grey Topper licensee Mr Alfred Thomas Hyslop, had his application for an on-licence renewal for the club turned down.

Mr M G Davies representing the police said Mr Hyslop was not a proper person to hold a licence after being fined more than £1000 during the last year for more than 40 offences that included hosting indecent exhibitions, selling to non members and to people under the age of 18.

Mr Hyslop told the committee that the membership of his club now totalled over 7500 but only 500 people could get in at one time. 'We have the finest club within 20 miles of Jacksdale. It was built from a pile of rubble at a cost of over £50,000 and could not have been done with bad running.'

Councillor Alan Strong came to Alf's support –

'If there was a popularity poll in the area Mr Hyslop would top the lot of us. His charity work has always been the same. He has given coal to pensioners during the winter months.'

The police were gunning for him, and at the end of the following statement, from a Chief Superintendent, we get an indication why.

'We've received complaints about urinating in doorways, fights outside the club and there was a serious assault on a police officer.'

Defending Alf Mr D. R. Sneath points out that he's been responsible in other ways and to give him one more chance. They refuse and it goes to Nottingham Crown court.

Ally: Young men have always had a punch up or three after a night out, go back as far as you like in this country, you're not going to stop that. We did have a bad element though, this area always had.

We sometimes had a problem with people selling drugs. Police got to know and sent some plain clothes officers down. They stuck out like a sore thumb with white shirts and ties on, the place cleared in five minutes.

They were more competent catching a tree thief though. Alf had bought all these conifers to go around the Topper grounds. This lad, who came in the club, had been uprooting some after a few beers. The cops came in, dragged him out and wailed his arse round back. Cops probably got a kick out of it.

We always got it in the neck from people. This woman across the road had a hairdressers, she was fed up with Topper regulars using her alley as a toilet.

She was remonstrating with me about one night, when I was on door.

'They don't do that honest,' I pleaded.

'They bloody do I can smell it, it stinks.'

'Could be drains.'

'Don't give me that and there's vomit as well.'

Just then this lad emerges from her alley doing up his flies.

'Look! There's one!'

She dragged him over by the ear.

'Him ere, he's always peeing in my alley Ally.'

'I'm not,' he protested.

'Don't gi mi that, what were yuh doing down there?'

'Thought of having a blow dry at hairdressers.'

'Come on, get it out, lets see if it's wet,' she said.

Tink: Yeah sounds like my mum.

Ally: It does annoy me, though, that it's now only remembered for the trouble. A young woman needed an operation on a knee to be able to walk properly. The Topper organised a meet the stars night with Jacksdale motorbike ace John Newbold. Along came his team mate Barry Sheen and Ron Haslam. They raised £6000 - £7000. It more than paid for the operation, they gave the rest to the hospital. Alf did a lot for charity. No one talks about those Topper days.

John Newbold.

Before Alf's day in court one of the Topper strippers is there before him. As was reported in the local press –

'A Sunday lunchtime striptease show at a Jacksdale club is the alternative to roast beef and Yorkshire pud.'

Stripper x - known as 'Rainbow' - is charged £10 for aiding and abetting an indecent exhibition. The court hears that on her first appearance she was wearing, a light blue see-through negligee over a black bra and pants, suspenders, belt and stockings and carried a whip, the second time it was an umbrella. On both occasions she took off all her clothes and each act contained parts that Det Sgt Burton judged indecent.

Mr Ian McClelland defending Rainbow pointed out she'd done her act all over the county including one for the police who didn't complain at the time. Three members of the Grey Topper audience are then asked to give their opinion. The first said the act was 'old fashioned', the next thought it was 'not very good at all,' the last described it as 'rubbish.' All charges are dropped.

Ally: It was called the Sunday Lunch Bunch, two strippers and a comedian. Plenty of blokes had a dried ring around their Sunday dinner plate when they got home. There was this one chap who, after paying his tote at the Welfare, would be waiting at the bus stop outside the Topper and start pleading with us to let him in on the cheap, so we relented.

'I'll just nip in for the pint, just see I have the one pint mind.'

'I will.'

Hours later his wife turns up.

'Tell im if he's not out in ten minutes his dinner will be on the compost heap at the top of the garden.'

I'd pretend to go and tell him, then go back and say to his wife –

'He says compost heap is the best place for your cooking.'

Fuming she storms in, sees her husband, plastered, head between the naked breasts of a stripper, and starts laying into him, dragging him out.

Then there was Bill Smith, he had these jam jar bottom specs. Just before the strippers came on he came up to the bar to get four pints in so he could get a prime position that no one could pinch if he had to rush to the toilet to er relieve himself.

At the end of the act he'd come wandering out with a wide smile on his face, but his specs had steamed up, so I'd remove them and clean them for him.

'Don't want yuh missus thinking you've been up to owt Bill.'

'Ah appen.'

We had all sorts, even an undertaker from Selston who'd come down, then buy a half of mild and sit with it all day.

'Isn't that a bit flat Natty?' I'd comment.

'No it wer dead when I got it, and I should know what dead is, I bury em all day.'

I used to call in at Fishlocks greengrocers to get some carrots for a pet rabbit. All his vegetables were a tuppence more than a greengrocers around the corner. I asked him how come, knowing they came from the same wholesalers.

'Have yuh not noticed that sign,' he said pointing to one hung above the counter. It said 'The sweetest of low prices, never the bitterness of low quality.'

I said 'I'll tell you what I'll do, if you've got any carrots going spare maybe I'll get you in free to see the sweetness of a stripper.'

At the Crown Court Alf was again successful in regaining his license.

*

The glam days were over and with it most of the current chart toppers appearing at the Topper. Many of the old 1960's favourites like The Merseybeats and Freddie and the Dreamers were still on the bill, but to the younger crowd these seemed passed their sell by date. Many of them were grebs, headbanging to the NWOBHM (New Wave Of British Heavy Metal) bands turning up at the Topper in 1975. Bands like Nutz (who have recently reformed and released a live album…recorded at the Grey Topper by Radio Trent), UFO and a young band from Birmingham called Judas Priest who were almost a resident band at the Grey Topper in 1975, playing 3 gigs.

Ashley Durose: I remember seeing Judas Priest, probably about 1975. Full light show, strobes, much 4 x12's, remote mixer desk etc, and the big gong - a sort of massive (5ft across?) cymbal that hung vertically at back of drums - and hardly anybody there, about 8 people. But they went through the full stage act with no complaints, guess getting paid anyway and treated it as a rehearsal? Later after becoming multi millionaires I saw a feature on them in *NME* I think, guess what was 'worst gig ever' according to them!

You could tell they were going to be big though. Halford a then shy young man but of course with that voice!

To other disaffected and bored teenagers, metal too seemed like old Topper hat, they were looking for a new sound, fashion and attitude to identify with. Down the Kings Road in London and on the pub rock circuit - where Dr Feelgood were now ripping it up - the kids had found it and were being inspired to do it themselves, they labelled the new movement punk.

The skins in the corner staring at the bar
The rude boys are dancing to some heavy heavy ska
It's getting so hot, people dripping with sweat
The punks in the corner, screaming like a jet
                    'Staring At The Rude Boys' – The Ruts

Autumn/winter 1979

'At Tibbshelf Miners Welfare is the splendid Riddings Brass Band.'

You really should take a look in the Topper Roy, I know Jacksdale's hard to find, but I'm sure someone will give you directions – Toyah next, three Top 10 singles, actress, future TV celebrity.

'Funny man Les Bryan is on at Newstead Miners Welfare.'

Go on spike up that hair, seminal punk band The Ruts are

on, they've already had a Top 10 record.

'Unwin Road Social Club – A welcome return for Wee Georgie Wheezer – comedy, song and Jolsen Impression.'

In the news –

Ripper Threat – Police Denial – 'Rumours that the Yorkshire Ripper is heading for Ashfield completely unfounded. Someone rang Kings Mill hospital claiming to be the Ripper saying a nurse is next on the list.

Miners accept 20% pay offer.

Bentink miners donate their 1 millionth tonne of coal to pensioners.

Arthur Hall given life sentence for the murder of Peter Thompson and Lorraine Underwood. Vera Thompson, Peter's mother, seeks contact with him through the spirit world.

*My mum and aunty go with her to see a spiritualist.

Drugs Alert – A dangerous drugs alert was issued yesterday after a burglary at Jacksdale chemists, the substance is white enamel.

166 Jacksdale residents sign a petition requesting the Grey Topper's liquor licence be revoked.

Bus Crew Ban To Beat Rowdies

Trent Buses drivers declare Jacksdale a no go area because of weekend trouble on buses. Until something is done about these hooligans the number 333 bus will not run through the village. 'We're not paid danger money and a conductor getting it, vomit, down his uniform was the last straw.' Says a company spokesperson.

Ally: We thought we could get around this by putting our own bus on. Only trouble was other people from other pubs and clubs would catch it as well. We spent all night dropping people off down these back streets.

'The so-called 'new fashion' of the skirt with split up the side is not very new. I wore them when I was young. We however were skinny thanks to wartime rations.

The very young lady who walked down the street with a skirt split nearly up to the waist (yuk too far) was so self-conscious that she looked and was grotesque.

Not many young ladies today are smart enough to wear any exciting fashions.'

I'd fallen under the spell of another girl who'd moved to the area. It's not that I fancied her or felt teenage kicks or anything, it was just deep admiration. When Liz Straw breezed, no she came in like a hurricane, into Mrs Hawley's English lesson things were never the same again.

I'd never met a girl like her, pink and red stripes in her hair, a tattered jacket with an anarchy symbol on the arm, black straight trousers, monkey boots and a left hook that could floor many a lad. The next surprise was she didn't go to the back of the class to slump apathetically on a chair. No, Liz sat in the middle of the front row, right in Mrs Hawley's face, staring at her intently. Then challenged everything she said. At first Mrs Hawley welcomed a debate, but when Liz started getting the upper hand, as regularly happened, and she was losing face, she'd tell Liz to shut up or leave.

'Don't you take away my freedom of speech, fascist,' Liz responded storming out.

Mrs Hawley saw herself as some sort of southern missionary come to enlighten us illiterate northern oiks. Her voice sounded like her parents had left her far too long in front of a radio listening to BBC announcers. She further alienated herself from us by turning up at school in a classic old Bentley, driven by her husband who would get out to open the door for her. Worst of all she constantly rammed D.H. Lawrence down our necks.

'You don't realise how lucky you are to have so much culture around here, D.H. Lawrence, Byron. Right on your doorstop, don't you realise, don't you care?'

'What abaht Brian Clough?' some lad put in.

I love D.H. Lawrence's books now, but back then, us punk kids from a council estate found his depiction of the local life boring and hard work.

'Dunt e goo all rahnd shop just to get some oats.' Was how one lad put it.

And anyway our grandad's told more entertaining and far funnier stories of past times in the area. And *A Kestrel For A Knave* - that another English teacher had given us to read – was much easier for us to identify with in 1979. I used to switch off from Mrs Hawley, stare out of the window, day dreaming up my own stories. I wrote one down for her one day. She just shoved my exercise book back in front of me with c- scrawled in red biro, no feedback, encouragement or anything (which one of us would end up getting a book published Mrs Hawley?)

So she was off again this day reading an extract from *Sons and Lovers*. When Liz tossed her book aside.

'Change the record.'

'To what may I ask?'

'Something that speaks to us about our isolation, being in a rut, all the bullshit around us like *The Catcher In A Rye*.'

'That's too subversive for my class Liz.'

'Dangerous you mean, we like subversive.'

'I really don't think so, and anyway I can't do an American accent.'

'You can't do our bloody accent, D.H. Lawrence spoke like

us yuh know, not some posh totty.'

I was snapped out of my daydream by this confrontation, this was brilliant, slamming my fist down on the table I shouted 'ANARCHEEeeee,' just as I did so, my voice broke.

Everyone looked in my direction, there was a moment of silence, then everyone was in fits of laughter. Liz, though, had me sit with her from then on, especially when she discovered what music I was into. All turned sour though, when I mentioned I might become a mod. She disowned me then after giving me a dead leg. Weeks later, after another teacher threw her out after losing an argument, Liz was expelled for starting a fire in the girls toilets.

Another extraordinary female punk was about to step onto the stage at the Grey Topper. When she was brave enough to come out of her dressing room.

Feff: We kept banging on the door, 'come out Toyah' or 'let us in, come on.'

Trained as an actress Toyah Wilcox also appeared in Derek Jarman's film *Jubilee* along side Adam Ant, before getting her band together.

When she came to the Topper she was on the big screen again playing 'Monkey' in the film adaptation of The Who's mod concept album *Quadrophenia*. Her mini album 'Sheep Farming In Barnet' had just been released.

Visually striking she was like magnet to a young punk.

Spike: She was stood at the bar so I went on over, took off my punk nappy - which was leopard skin one side and bright green tartan on the other - and asked her to sign it. Then I thought I'd chance my luck and ask her for a kiss. Boy did she give me one, we were stood there snogging away, then this guy turns up, annoyed look on his face and drags her away. Don't know if he was her boyfriend or not, he looked pissed off though.

Feff: I became one of her biggest fans and got to know her. She used to put me and my mate Sid on the guest list at gigs. We'd go in early to watch them do a soundcheck, hang around with them and even played tick. I know it sounds daft playing tick with Toyah but we did.

We went to one gig in Coventry and the back stage party. When Toyah heard we had nowhere to stay - we were just going to doss down in the railway station - she invited us to crash in their tour van, then travel to Birmingham with them. She was making a documentary there and we appeared in that as well.

A week after the Toyah concert and Spike wasn't so confident in approaching the charismatic singer of The Ruts, Malcolm Owen.

Spike: I was like fuck'n'ell Malcolm Owen. I'd brought my copy of 'Babylon's Burning' along hoping to get him to autograph it, but I just didn't have the bottle to go ask him. Debbie Fletcher from Ripley knew him, so she took me by the hand and introduced us. He was great and signed the record cover with the message -

'Don't be shy Spike – Malcolm Owen.'

The Ruts were one of the last but arguably greatest of the punk groups to play the Grey Topper. Championed by Radio 1's John Peel their second single the explosive and brilliant 'Babylon's Burning' smashed into the Top 10.

Like The Clash they added elements of reggae to their music. 'Staring at the Rude Boys' was a direct fuck off to racists causing trouble at their gigs. Live they were raw and fast and in Owen had a livewire front man.

The Ruts (l-r): Segs Jennings, Malcolm Owen, Paul Fox, Dave Ruffy.

Feff: Malcolm Owen pogoed about the stage telling us to spit at him 'Go on get one in my gob,' he shouted.

Stephen Fletcher: I think they finished with 'Human Punk'. I can remember, at the end of the gig, all the band jumped out into the crowd. The audience was mainly lads as you'd probably expect. I was part of a circle of about 8 or 10 that were jumping about to the 'punk stuff' that was being played after the gig and Malcolm Owen came and jumped in amongst us, pogoing etc...

Mick Clark: Looking back in hindsight The Ruts were very special, we didn't know that Malcolm Owen would die less than a year later. At the Topper, at the end of the gigs, everyone who was not local would fuck off home after the gig, the locals would stay behind for the disco. Very often bands would stay and unwind with a drink, it was a surreal time talking with your heroes who'd been on *Top of the Pops* the week before! It's easy to say this now but I had a chat with Malcolm Owen at the bar and he was a great guy. We went to see them a few days later at the Sandpiper in Nottingham and he said 'hello mate' to me from the stage - a big thing for me as an 18-year-old. R.I.P. Malcolm.

The Ruts were at their peak at the time of their Grey Topper gig; a Top 40 band, an acclaimed album out and a tour of America planned. But Malcolm Owen's sad decline into heroin addiction had already begun. Soon he was lying to the rest of the band after failing to turn up for rehearsals. When he did, he was strung out and disappearing into the toilets for half an hour at a time to take the smack he'd sneaked in by hiding it in secret compartments of his shoes.

As a last resort, and as an effort to try and shock him off the drug, the rest of The Ruts split the band. At first it seemed to work, Owen booked himself into rehab, and on release joined the band in the studio to lay down the vocals for new tracks. The following Monday - July 14th 1980 - he was found dead in his bath from a heroin overdose. Malcolm Owen was only 26. His life was over and - despite the rest of the band soldiering on briefly as Ruts D.C. – that of one of the best of the second wave of punk bands.

Listen to the stripped back, raw power of their *Peel Sessions* album and it still sounds fresh and exciting to this day, a clear sign that the band had the potential to go on to even greater heights. Malcolm Owen's lyrics to 'H-Eyes' – the b-side to 'In A Rut' – had been prophetic – 'You're so young, you take smack for fun – It's gonna screw your head, you're gonna wind up dead.'

When the UK Subs returned to the Topper - a few weeks after The Ruts - it was the end of an era. Alf, under pressure from residents, the council and police, announced he was banning punk groups playing the Topper. Perhaps he had a modern solution in mind. As one night soon afterwards mod revivalists the Merton Parkas took to the stage.

The group was short-lived, having just the one single that reached the Top 40 'You Need Wheels.' But they did have Mick Talbot in their ranks, who later tasted pop stardom when teaming up with The Jam's Paul Weller to form The Style Council.

They didn't have much success with the Topper punks either, who were determined to make a last stand for their cause.

Alf soon says he's sick of battles between mods and punks and neither type of group will play the Topper again. In a further effort to save his club he secures the signatures of 700 regulars demanding the club stay open as opposed to the 166 who demanded it close.

There's more dismay for the punks when Marsy, one of the originals, is seen wearing a parka.

Something Better Change

The times they were a changing and in early 1976 an ice cream van pulled into the Grey Topper car park playing a discordant tune.

Jet Black – The Stranglers: I can assure you that the ice cream van was indeed the mode of transport for the Grey Topper gig, perhaps the only one in rock 'n' roll history? It had been a legacy from an earlier business enterprise.

What did the rest of The Stranglers think of it and, when on tour, did anyone ever come up asking for an ice cream?

Jet Black: The other guys had their initial laugh - like everyone always does - then realized it was the ice cream van, or walk! And oh yes we had many a person coming up and saying 'any free samples.'

Jet Black's legendary ice cream van – just don't go knocking on the window asking for Mr Softy it's full of Stranglers!

The Stranglers new sound struck a chord with some of the Topper crowd, even if the group themselves were non-too impressed with their fee of £75 (for the whole band). According to one person who got in touch with me about the Topper, The Stranglers apparently wrote '(Get a) Grip (On yourself)' about it?

Jet Black: It is just about feasible. At the time of the Grey Topper gig we were un-signed. 1976 was a gruelling year, 193 gigs all over the place. We were on the road most of the time but certainly built up a huge following. Initially thousands of people hated us! We were rejected wherever and whenever we played, always abused and often not paid or disputed. It was a kind of hell that in a perverted kind of way, we relished.

The fact is, that amid all those thousands who hated us, there must have been a handful who were inclined to the opposite, and over a period of 2/3 years became a central mass which - upon release of our first album, suddenly, and I mean suddenly, it all changed on one particular night - we were applauded. That one night was when we supported Patti Smith at the Roundhouse. Well, the smash hit album at the end of that period was a kind of sweet revenge/justice kind of thing.

Tony Oglesby: Me and my mate really didn't know what to expect when we saw 'The Stranglers' advertised at the Topper, but the first time I heard the baseline from 'Peaches' has always stuck in the memory since that night. This is really different I thought as they went through a very strong melodic first set, which featured keyboards heavily. Of course, much of this would come to be released in 1977 - as these guys must have been on the verge of landing a recording contract - with 'Peaches' reaching the Top 10 despite being banned.

They were up against it that night though, with an audience consisting of mainly second generation Teddy Boys. As the set wore on chants of 'play some rock and roll' started and when they came back for the second set they started with 'Good Golly Miss Molly' and 'Great Balls of Fire.' A good example of playing to the crowd I think. Who wouldn't though, as intimidating as

The Stranglers were, they were no match for the Notts and Derby border Teds.

What was the driving force to give up a business and start a band, what were the influences to come up with The Stranglers down on the street or 'down in the sewer' sound?

Jet Black: I just woke up one day and said to myself, 'what am I doing in this business, what ever happened to my desire to be in music'. I had been a prolific amateur and semi-pro in my late teens and beyond.

There was no discussion or format about our sound, it just came out the way it came out, accident. We were the band all the punk bands came to see. It was our aggressive music at the time which attracted many, but that was born out of a frustration with the struggle to survive the rigours of the music industry. Today things are very different. We are in the agreeable position of being able to play wherever and whenever we want.

How did the punk before punk name The Stranglers come about?

Jet Black: We all lived in this rented house. After each day's rehearsal and/or song writing sessions there was usually time for relaxation - and, over a period of some weeks, there seemed to be a near-daily 'strangling.' This was either fictional - by way of some TV film or play (Hitchcock's *Frenzy* was doing the rounds at around this time) or actual - in newspapers and other media reports. The word 'stranglers' or 'strangling' was so omnipresent around this period that it began to be adopted as a comic reference in the house.

And it was after an early Guildford gig, and a disastrous one at that - everything that could have gone wrong did - that JJ happened to say, 'the stranglers have really done it this time,' a jokey reference to the band's performance that night. It's

141

generally considered that this immortal line was the origin of the name. It was, of course, in jest, but since no alternative was ever agreed upon, it eventually stuck.

When did you become aware of the scene changing, punk bubbling up in London?

Jet Black: First inkling was when we became aware that we were following a band called the Sex Pistols around the circuit - and they/us – and they were being associated with the word, and genre, known as 'punk.' We were also aware that a number of the people who became leading figures in this new movement had been front row attendees at many of our shows.

But did you ever consider yourselves a 'punk' band?

Jet Black: No, we didn't consider ourselves a 'punk' band, it's just a label. You must remember that unlike all of our contemporaries, we had been touring Britain for three years before anyone heard the word 'punk'. No, of course we were never a 'punk' band. What on earth is punk about 'Golden Brown', 'Always the Sun', or even, 'Hanging Around'? However, this didn't stop the entire news industry calling us 'punk'. It's something we never acknowledged, or denied. And it undoubtedly was a great assistance to the development of our career, although there was a down side to it. We got banned all over the place, and have spent 30 years trying to put the record straight.

*

Eddie – The Vibrators: Our first gig was supporting The Stranglers at Hornsey Art College North London in 1976.

The Vibrators were one of the original punk bands, they supported the Sex Pistols at the 100 Club and performed at the legendary Punk Rock Festival. By the time they played the Grey

Topper in spring 1977 they had already recorded a session for Radio 1's John Peel show and released three singles 'We Vibrate', 'Pogo Dancing,' and 'Bad Times.'

Eddie – The Vibrators: I know we couldn't find the Grey Topper, it was this mining village in the middle of nowhere wasn't it? Yeah, we ended up lost in this field, then on some council estate where we had to ask directions.

I've got visions of this van pulling up and these punks asking some old timer were the Grey Topper is and the reaction when they say they're Vibrators.

Eddie: We'd been on the road all day, when we got there I just crashed on the grass and went to sleep.

I enquire about their tour van, as it's becoming a regular point of interest.

Eddie: We had an old Transit crew bus and a Bedford van brought from 'Gothic Electricals,' to carry the gear and roadies, hence the 'Gothic Horror tours.' It had a top speed of 45 mph, you could get it to go faster if you freewheeled it down a hill. Also it broke down a lot and was a bitch to start in the cold. Our tour of Holland in Jan 77 was about minus ten degrees every day and we'd get about ten parking tickets a day.

I wonder what the Topper crowd's reaction was to this new sound?

Eddie: There was a real buzz from the crowd. I think they appreciated we were just getting back to rock 'n' roll roots and playing loud, fast, rebellious music that was trying to say something. If it didn't work, well, at least we had tried.

Most early 70's music was glam stuff, which was the odd

good song with silly clothes or endless dreary folk or prog rock with everyone wanting to sound like The Band. Dull isn't the word.

The Vibrators had just finished touring with Iggy Pop (with Bowie guesting in his band doing backing vocals and playing keyboards) when they arrived in Jacksdale.

Eddie: Iggy and Bowie were great but we'd lost loads of money. The thing that sticks in my mind is these loony Bowie fans would turn up at the hotels with full Aladdin insane makeup and clothes asking to talk to David. The crew made more money than us, in Manchester they sold about ten beer cans that Bowie had had on his keyboard, and 3 or 4 chairs he sat on to his fans for about £10 a time.

I ask what it was like to be there at one of the most famous gigs in the history of rock. November 6th 1975. A bunch of scruffy kids had blagged the support spot to Bazooka Joe (with Stuart Goddard aka Adam Ant). They called themselves the Sex Pistols, a punk revolution was born.

Eddie: To be honest I thought they were so-so that night. I remembered Johnny Rotten as this kid with holes in his jumper asking for Stooges records when I was a DJ there, and then changing the lyrics from 'love' to 'hate' in the Small Faces song. He was an amazing character, always the one with something to say.

I helped carry all the Sex Pistols gear downstairs because someone had broken the lift. John (Rotten) and Steve went to fetch their amp from the rehearsal room on Denmark Street, which was next to St Martins. While they were gone, me and John Ellis started jamming with Glen Matlock and Paul Cook. I sang, believe it or not, 'Bonie Moronie,' 'Johnny B Goode' and some other songs.

Did he think he'd still be in The Vibrators all these years later?

Eddie: Yeah I did actually, well maybe not 30 years on, but the buzz is still there. Next month we're touring America and Brazil, that's got to be better than cleaning a blocked drain or being stuck in an office for a living.

I go back to 1976 and the day The Vibrators played the Punk Rock Festival at the 100 Club. Was that the moment when he felt the movement had truly arrived?

Eddie: Yeah it all came together at the 100 Club, we were all there, The Pistols, The Clash, The Dammed, Buzzcocks, Siouxsie. Punk had arrived and our efforts were starting to pay off.

It was a chaotic mess though, and the downside was the Sid Vicious (he played drums for Siouxsie and the Banshees at the event) glassing incident. He had a screw loose. Taking a kid out to an ambulance with her eye cut open, which she was left blinded in, was the worst. That wasn't what punk was about.

BABYLON'S BURNING

Spike: You see, the punks got the blame, as usual, when the lad lost an eye, but none of us were there, we'd gone down Derby to see The Clash.

> This town is coming like a ghost town
> All the clubs have been closed down
> This place is coming like a ghost town
> Too much fighting on the dance floor
> > 'Ghost Town' – The Specials.

1980's

'Ashfield doesn't have any nuclear shelters. I am wondering if any sub committee has been formed to work out plans for Ashfield's public in the event of nuclear attack.

I would expect a leaflet at least on the best place to run to, school etc. It would be a good idea to have the under stairs cubby hole strengthened.'

In the news -

Grim job crisis – 'Ashfield's industrial grey area is turning an ominous shade of black.'

400 people laid off at Metal Box if steel strike continues.

Shock closure of Jacksdale pipe works, 200 jobs to go.

200 school ancillary workers in Ashfield are to lose their jobs under Tory controlled Education Committee cutback.

Jacksdale favourite gets the axe. Frank Revell, crossing warden for

25 years, victim of cutbacks. Head of road safety officer says 'cuts had to be made and that's that.' They only offer redundancy of £2 for every year he has worked there.

*We loved Mr Revell as kids at the junior school, come his birthday he'd be swamped under with cards. He was always saying 'Confucius say' then come out with something funny, until mad axe woman Thatcher chopped off his head and stole his lollipop.

Strike call to beat Tory employment bill. MP Frank Haynes warns about hard won union rights being taken away.

'The government is gunning for you. I appeal to the whole trade union movement, stand together like the miners did in 1972. We can bring Thatcher down if we go about it the right way.'

High cost of fuel causing elderly to turn heating down.

Young Sutton boys mill around with swastikas on their arms.

A 61-year-old granny goes punk, dyes her hair blue and green, wears a dog collar, bondage trousers and chains to raise money for charity.

Killer dog virus sweeps the area. Which intensifies one council estates war on packs of scavenging dogs. Vicious fights spill into gardens. 'They howl all night, mess on the grass and now they're going crazy over a bitch, the poor things only a puppy,' comments one angry resident.

Heavy rockers, punks and mods battle on the streets. So its obvious to one local reporter what the cause and effect of Ashfield's problems are. Not Thatcherism.

'More trouble today is caused through pop music and the likes and dislikes of the singer.'

Jacksdale Neglect Claim.

The forgotten people of Ashfield were brought to the attention of the county council at their meeting on Thursday. 'The streets have not been kerbed since 1928 and nothings been done about the floods,' said councillor Taylor.

STOP PRESS – One, one mind you, piece of good news. Council

plan to beat Jacksdale floods.

'For several years heavy rains have caused floods along Selston Road. Now there are plans to divert the water through a channel and a box culvert.'

Back to the bad news- Jacksdale's Community Centre delayed for two years.

I'm being a lazy sod, slumped on the settee at home watching the television, I'm bored with that, bored with everything and generally being an adolescent pain in the arse. No one is more pissed off with me than my sister. Being at college and uni, living in student digs has made her fiercely independent and none too happy with the way I allow mam to do everything for me. We've just had tea and she's demanded I do the dishes. I reluctantly say I will to shut her up, but have no intention of doing so. Grabbing my jacket I try to sneak out of the back door.

'Oi where you going?'

'Out.'

'Not until you've done the dishes you're not.'

I stick two fingers up to her and head for the door. Elaine picks up the rolling pin (mam was using to make an apple pie for Sunday dinner) and hurls it at me. It somersaults through the air, narrowly misses my head and embeds in the door (even my dad's best DIY efforts can't patch the hole that's there for years). I'm legging it down the street.

Banned from the only poxy, crumbling night club we know the 'yowf club,' a proper modern one still two years away with the hold up with the community centre, we wander the streets bored out of our tiny minds. If we're lucky, some older passing youth will get us some alcohol from the off license.

Then we can go off to the only place where we can do what we want to, away from prying eyes and busybodies. The old, derelict steel works just over the canal in Ironville. The place is vast, one of the shops must be the length of Wembley Stadium. Thousands worked there at one time, not now, we've got it all to ourselves – for a while – an underground playground.

We can vent our frustration smashing parts of it up. We've turned one of the smaller shops into our own leisure centre though. A make-do skateboard park, and a five-a-side football pitch with the nets sprayed onto a wall with Day-Glo paint. For illumination we start little fires around the edges of the shop.

Our enjoyment doesn't last long. A shout goes up, the police have been spotted at the gates, that are blocked with rubble to stop gypsies moving onto the site, giving us time to hide, but not put the fires out.

They come in with torches, but the place is so big, with a maze of old offices, that they can never find us. A beam of light does enter the one where we are all crouched in, but they don't come any nearer. They do shout a warning however.

'We'll be back later, if we catch any of you, expect time in a borstal for attempted arson.'

We can't understand why they're picking on us. We go somewhere that's away from annoying people outside their homes, to a place that's going to be pulled down anyway and still they won't leave us alone.

In despair and anger we pile more and more debris onto the fires, conifer branches from the trees outside really get them flaring up, soon the flames are licking the roof, we all run back to Jacksdale. From there you can see the orange glow from the building and sirens in the distance. We don't care, the Ironville lot will get the blame as usual.

Outside the chippy – across from the Topper – a youth, a mod, is sat on a gleaming Lambretta scooter, which has an array of spotless wing mirrors. We gather round it, ask if we can sit on it. But he warns if we touch it or as much as put a smear on one of the mirrors he'll 'break our faces.'

We can't wait until Saturday when we can escape Jacksdale and catch the 333 bus to Nottingham (before they stop running through the village once the Topper doors open). There we come across an amazing sight. Hundreds of mods, in a long line, are coming down the opposite escalator in the Broadmarsh Shopping Centre. One at the front, for what reason I know not, except to annoy people, is carrying a dead rabbit, its eyes gouged out, he swings this from side to side in rhythm to the tune they're loudly humming - Booker T and the MG's 'Green Onions' part of the soundtrack to *Quadrophenia*.

Excitedly we start following them. They head towards Slab Square and the steps of the council house. Everyone knows this is where the punks hang out and it's all going to kick off. It does, and the mods, who outnumber the punks, seem to be coming out on top, then the police move in. Impressed we go to the Victoria Centre market and buy fish tail parkas.

At the Topper Alf was having to do battle with punks and mods, and, as ever, the police, council, magistrates and residents. Having secured the signatures of over 700 regulars petitioning to keep the place open, he must have felt he would again come out victorious. Then an incident happened that would cause his dream to come crashing down.

You never lose a bad reputation. The Grey Topper was now infamous for trouble and still attracting gangs of youths who wanted to indulge in it. One such was a gang from Sutton who had a few scores to settle with the Topper crowd. One night they donned motorbike helmets, picked up baseball bats and headed down into the valley. Heading this way in the opposite direction was a gang from Eastwood. Jacksdale youths would be caught up in the middle.

Feff: I think it was The Clash's *London Calling* tour, they were playing in Derby so we all headed down there. We either couldn't get in or it had been cancelled, so we headed back to Jacksdale.

Spike: By the time we got there it was all over with and the police had just turned up. Cork was in the chippy and he got arrested because he was one of the Topper punks and was sent down for 18 months. He'd had nothing to do with it.

We sent Cork a Christmas card in borstal, that we'd taken in the Topper for all his punk friends to sign, punkettes put red lipstick kisses all over it and we added beer stains and sellotaped on a squashed chip complete with ketchup – essence of the Topper! He opened it Christmas Day – after having had to do a run down the beach at 6.a.m. – it made his day, but cry, even though he was a tough lad, it made him think of what he was missing. Soon we'd all be missing it, for ever.

Several local youths, who *were* involved in the battle that lead to a lad losing an eye after being beaten with a fence post, were also given sentences.

Snoz: It was vicious, you had to grab anything you could, bricks, sticks and bottles to defend yourself.
*Snoz would be sent to borstal for his involvement.

It was the death knell for the Grey Topper.

Perhaps knowing the writing was on the wall Alf proposed turning the building into a community centre. No one wanted to know any more. But he did get unexpected support from an opinion column in the local press –

'Selston Parish Council should take advantage of Alfred Hyslop's public spirited offer to turn his Grey Topper night club into a community centre. Over the years Mr Hyslop has come in for his share of criticism, but it cannot be denied that he has tried to bring entertainment to a quiet backwater and when trouble has reared its head, for various reasons, he was always prepared to take preventative measures.

At a time of cost pruning it would seem a splendid idea to provide a much needed community focal point for young and old alike using existing premises.'

It fell on deaf ears, leaving the club to go through a slow

painful death. A bierkeller was tried but that was out of place and out of time. A sparse number of groups still appeared, only crap one's that only Roy Booker would take any pleasure in. Many had apt names for the club's plight – Weapons Of Peace, Dirty Work, Bleeding Hearts, Low Profile, Strange Days, Blazer.

As did the name of the last group of any note to play the Grey Topper – B-Movie. A local band formed in Mansfield, who made their debut at Sutton baths, they heralded a new style of music about to hit the charts - the New Romantics.

B-Movie.

Steve Hovington - B-Movie: It was at an early stage in our career. We were then managed by a local miner called John 'Yank' Fritchley, who luckily had a trailer on the back of his car so we could play further a field than the Mansfield area. Jacksdale was quite exotic for us.

It was at that time when we were starting to wear eyeliner and glittery ties and dying our hair bright orange so we were always wary of the local skinheads. We actually supported The Angelic Upstarts, believe it or not, at The Sandpiper in Nottingham. We'd play anywhere then but there was always the threat of violence especially in places like Lincoln and Derby. We were honoured to play the Topper especially after our idols Ultravox and Simple Minds had played there.

Perhaps if Alf had known the pop future he could have weathered the storm. Duran Duran and Spandau Ballet could have been booked early in their careers. And you couldn't picture their fans, prancing about in frilly shirts quoting Lord Byron, being any problem. Maybe they might occasionally hit people with their handbags.

The Smiths could have played there with youths doing little damage swatting each other with gladioli. Or my crowd a few years later, the indie kids (yes I was short lived as a mod. How could a scruffy, penniless dropout, who hung out in dusty factories be clean cut. That image didn't express the way I felt), we were too busy shoegazing to look up and throw a punch.

It was not to be. One night sirens could be heard racing along Selston Road and coming to a halt outside the Grey Topper....

...Malc had leant forward, mischievous glint in his eye.

'Of course it came to an end with the fire, got to be careful what I say, don't want to say owt incriminating but it was a bit'....he wiggles his hand from side to side as a sign of dodgy.

'I was there when it started let me say that,' he continues a wry smile on his face.

How did it start then?

'Well some reckon a record player was left on and overheated.'

'What was it playing "Fire", "Come on Baby Light My Fire," "Great Balls Of Fire?'

'He, he, not sure, could have been, what was that punk song....Babylon's Burning.'

Spike: I remember coming home from work that night, Alf, still in his suit, his wife and kids were sat on the wall across from the Topper, sad looks on their faces as the fireman tried to put out the fire. All they owned scattered around them.

Maybe Spike didn't need to feel that sorry for them.

Malc: I took six bags of cash out of the place for Alf that night. We both went back in later to check the damage, and knowing the dream was over emptied the optics and slept on the pool tables. I locked up for the last time next day.

Not everyone realised - or wanted to accept - that the Topper was closed. Having gone on his usual route of pubs on Sunday, one regular headed there hoping, in his inebriated state, that the pumps would still be on.

Marsy: I somehow found my way in. Stumbled in the dark to the bar and waited to get served. Of course I never did, but I couldn't find my way out and fell over and went to sleep. About seven thirty next morning I found the exit, fell over the perimeter wall, through the conifers and landed on the pavement. All these people at the bus stop, waiting to go to work and school, were pissing themselves. I was black, covered head to toe in soot.

Several years later Malc got a call from Alf.
'Do you want to start again Malc?'
'Start what?'
'A club.'
'Don't you think we're getting bit old for that now?'
'We're old dogs we know all the tricks?'

He talked of buying the Topper back, but the council were having none of that. So he hoped to take over the Tin Hat at Selston, making it similar to the Topper. It never got off the ground and then he became ill. Alf died of leukaemia a year later.

*

The fire wasn't the end for the Picture Palace building. Like some mutant phoenix rising from the flames Woody's 2 opened in 1983. Those square residents, who strove to have the Topper closed down, probably wished they'd kept their mouths shut and backed Alf's plea to turn the place into a community centre after this bastard child of the Topper and Woody's club in Ripley was born.

There were no live acts but - with the advent of video – the music shown on the mutli-screens and pumping out the DJ's speakers was loud and in your face. The ghosts of Topper past - Adam and the Ants, Simple Minds, The Specials, Eurythmics (all of which had now become million record selling bands) and punk - haunted the place. Not many of the teenagers trying to look good on the dance floor (including myself and failing) realised the real thing had stood and performed on that very spot.

Although there was nothing of the scale of the punk riots, trouble did kick off most weekends. This wasn't averted too well by the owner Steve 'woody' Woodward, who saw himself as an East Midlands Robert De Niro (there was a resemblance), showing the violent, blood-spattered final twenty minutes of

Taxi Driver on the video screens nearly every weekend, just before closing time. Square residents tried to get it closed down. Woody had to fight for his licence.

The thing was, though, Woody was his worst enemy. Perhaps possessed by the evil Topper spirits unleashed by Judas Priest or maybe he'd just watched too many De Niro films, he was the one who lead to the clubs demise in the 1990's. Backed by bouncers he inflicted GBH on a troublesome customer and was sent down and the club closed.

The building had the ignominious fate of ending up as a lampshade factory. That too fell to the Topper curse, the lights definitely went out for the last time when the business folded and the place was again boarded up.

2010 –

Nowhere man please listen. Maybe you're right. Jacksdale, a pleasant, thriving, safe and nice to place to live in. Situated in a forgotten corner of Nottinghamshire that no one can find and no one really wants to anymore. Two of the very few buildings with character and architectural merit allowed to be demolished, deemed to be blots on the landscape because of their chequered - and at times none too pleasant - history. To be replaced by yet another supermarket and housing for townie commuters, who never socialise in the few remaining pubs and are only seen when polishing their cars on the driveway on Sunday mornings.

The only life and colour in the village now to be seen are in the many hanging baskets dotted along the streets. The Flowerpot man's vision of creating *Pleasantville*. Those of you who have seen that film know what the result of that false idealism is. I prefer what the famous soul groups called 'Jacksonville.'

There's still no sign of the time capsule, and Ally had told me that they also buried a load of gas bottles there. The Topper just might go out with a bang yet, it might put some life back into the village - Vive Le Rock.

Epilogue
I Predict A Riot

Yeah vive le rock. I wished I'd have been there. How many times have I said that to myself since starting this Grey Topper project? I mean I'd just missed out, there had been me, baby punk, buying records by The Members, The Ruts, The Specials and UK Subs, my heroes, and they'd been playing live in my village at the time! All these years of having to listen to the Topper punks bragging about those legendary nights. But what if....

I couldn't write this story and not be swamped by nostalgia and possessed by the spirit of the Topper and owner Alf. So I had the idea early on. Build it again and maybe, just maybe, they'd come again. What if I could put on a Grey Topper concert and bring some of the groups back to Jacksdale?

Only the Grey Topper had been demolished of course, the Portland would have been an ideal substitute but...demolished. The Social Club? You can't get in there unless you've been a member for at least 10 years (which I've not), have a key fob and an encrypted password. It's easier to be accepted into the Freemasons.* The old Miners Welfare (now imaginatively renamed 'The Dale Club') would be the ideal venue because of the size of its rooms. But I came out in a cold sweat thinking about having to approach the committee with the plan for a 'Grey Topper Punks Reunited' night and didn't really want to give them the pleasure in turning me down, which I guessed would be the inevitable outcome.

That just left 3 back street pubs on Palmerston Street. All of which would be too small, then again the Royal Oak had just had an extension built – so you could get about 100 people in there – and was run by Byrnie who I'd known for years and used to be a punk? He was a big fan of the UK Subs too?

---

*BG – Written before Geordie took over and had the sense to do away with the membership and make it 'welcome to all,'....apart from Manchester United fans probably, damn.

The UK Subs were one band I could conceivably get to do a concert. Although lead singer Charlie Harper wasn't the youngest of punks in 1979, his band – with several line-ups – had outlived them all (and have just won the BBC 6 Music 'Punk Rock World Cup' knocking out The Clash and Sex Pistols along the way and beating Stiff Little Fingers in the final) It seems he's been on the road non-stop for 30 years.

He was a mate now as well, virtually, we'd been swapping emails for months since I first contacted him about the Grey Topper (although he was too out of it in 1979 to remember much about the place). Charlie agrees straight away when I put it to him, this is in September but - like most groups - the UK Subs are booked up for the year, so we settle on May the following year.

I do find a Nottingham punk venue who do want to put a Topper night on, Junktion 7, then after talking to the owner Adrian I discover he was a Topper punk, not only that, he was also part of a crowd of Ripley punks I briefly hung about with when I was 16!

Everything seems to be falling into place, just a few more negotiations to do with the groups, booking fees, etc and it really could be on. There is a strong desire gnawing away inside of me however to get a punk gig back on in the village, give something back to the Topper crowd. Ok and maybe ruffle a few feathers as well, and when the Royal Oak landlord Byrnie tells me it's his dream to have the UK Subs play his pub, a mohican topped devil pogos excitedly on my shoulder, I can't resist.

I reluctantly phone Adrian at Junktion 7 and thank him for his support but hope he realises what the sentiment of bringing one of the Topper punk bands of 79 back to Jacksdale means.

We could only safely get about 100 people in the Royal Oak, one headline band – which will be the UK Subs – and possibly a local band as support. I ok it with Charlie, he's fine to play in a small pub 'just make sure the PA's adequate,' he says. He can fit the gig in on May 17th, between a tour of Australia, New

Zealand, Japan and a punk festival in Amsterdam.

Great! Byrnie and me shake on it and he suggests we leave the preparations for the gig until after Christmas – it's the beginning of December – I'm happy with this, I'm ready for a break from the Topper project now, I've been working on it since May. I've written the story (apart from this last chapter), got the web site up and running, now the 'Grey Topper Punks Reunited' concert is on, the capacity is small but it's in the village and hopefully there will be some profit for Cancer research. I sit back satisfied and look forward to Christmas and the New Year....

It effects 1 in 3 they say, so, far too many of you out there will have been through it, either battled it yourself or watched a loved one suffer horribly. It came like a mortar out of the blue. Dad had been fine, been working hard – with others – on the renovations for my brother and sister-in-laws new house, until stomach pains meant he had to take a rest, then he turned a yellow colour and when I saw him, saw his eyes, I knew, even before he went for tests, I knew, I'd seen a friend's dad in the same condition a few years before who died of it, no one had to tell me and I kept it to myself and cried at home. Dad was diagnosed with terminal cancer in the week before Christmas and just few days before his and mum's Golden Wedding Anniversary on the 22nd.

Although still in hospital dad's determined to get out for the anniversary party that was to take place at the welfare. We say we ought to cancel, that people will understand but dad will have none of it. On the night he's there all full of smiles and dignity. We all try to be brave over Christmas, hide our sadness in front of him, but it's very difficult, dad's the one who's brave and never complains once. He even insists we watch the classic episode of *Steptoe and Son* (repeated on BBC 2) when Albert is confined to bed and gets Harold running all over the shop and seeing to his every need. Dad warns mum that's what's she's in for between laughter every time Albert's shouts 'oh and HARRROOOLLLD.'

161

I spend Christmas dazed and confused and pretty fucked up. I'm walking my parent's dog around the village one night, it's so strange going through this at this time of the year, all the Christmas lights and through windows I could see families having a good time, weird, I felt outside of everything, like Dickens's ghosts of Christmas past, present and future rolled into one....

The 'Grey Topper Punks Reunited' concert gives me something to focus on during dad's illness, the only real regret I have - as the overheads mount - is that the venue isn't bigger so I could make more for Cancer Research UK.

Then as time goes by I start to get real doubts, the spectre of the 'Black Horse' has raised it ugly head for the first time. But I still go ahead and book hotel rooms for the UK Subs, hire a PA, customise the tour posters Charlie has sent me, print the tickets and, not wanting to leave it any longer (its March now) put them on sale. Topper punk Sam Pilgrim has shifted nearly 10 in a week, Spike asked for the same amount, people are ringing the Oak when the tour date goes up on the UK Subs web site.

Then Byrnie tells me he's reluctantly got to cancel the gig, there's been a break in at his pub, recent trouble, and with the news of the UK Subs return spreading like wild fire, residents associations and the police are putting the pressure on.. I wonder if he's being haunted by the 'Black Horse' too. I've now only 7 weeks to find a new venue and set it all up again.

162

I'm depressed on Sunday, I don't need this shit with the gig with dad the way he is. We now know his cancer is inoperable and chemotherapy is looking doubtful too, if so he has only months, but he's being strong, taking everything in his stride. Inspired by his courage I wake up on Monday morning a different person. I'll get this fucking concert on and raise money to help fight that horrible disease too, see if I don't, I tell myself. I even pluck up the courage to approach the Miners Welfare about putting it on.

After a shot of Dutch courage I roll up my posters and gather my tickets and stride on over there (had to be there at 9.30 a.m. sharp, but it's only about 100 yards from my house) I'm shitting myself that I'd be straight up before the committee. Oh shite! They had a more fearsome reputation than the *Dragon's Den*. I was determined to make a good pitch though.

I felt a little bit at ease when I walk in as the cleaner knew me – 'Ey up Tony duck' she said sweeping up the nights discarded bingo tickets.

'Ey up Sharon duck,' I replied.

And I'm pleasantly surprised when I walk into an office in the corner, there's not a host of furrowed brows and disdainful old eyes staring at me through a cloud of pipe smoke. Two ladies greet me with pleasant nods, the first I know, Enid, she's related to my sister-in-law (big deal, everybody is related to everyone else down here, no I didn't say in-breds) and seems to be the entertainment manager.

'You've got the UK Subs to come here!' Says a woman at her side. Then tells me she was at the Topper when they played there in 1979 and would like to go to this one too and knows others who would as well.

The deal was done and I paid my deposit for the room, they promised to put up posters, which I thought funny, UK Subs 'Warhead' posters going up in the Welfare!

Great it's back on, and at a place that can hold up to 200 people, I'm pretty confident I can get around 150 to 200 to come see the UK Subs, that's about their average audience for smaller out of the city venues. If so I would make about £500 plus – after overheads - for Cancer Research UK. I'll have to pull my finger out, though, there is now only just over six weeks to the gig. I spend the rest of the day redesigning posters and reprinting 200 tickets.

Dad – who's looking and feeling the best he has since first being diagnosed with cancer (after being put on steroids to build him up to start a course of chemotherapy, which he can now try and wants to) is chuffed too about it being on at the welfare. His old sense of humour has returned too.

'Which group is it you've got?' He asks.

'The UK Subs, a one time Top 40 punk band who played the Topper twice in 1979. They've been just about touring non stop for 30 years.'

'Yeah? Should have bloody learned how to play by now then?' He replies before going off to have kick about in the garden with his grandchildren - our Alex and Christy. With the gig seemingly to be definitely on, and a glimmer of hope for dad, I feel happy for the first time in months.

It doesn't last, there's a message on my answer phone. It's Enid from the welfare, apparently there have been rumblings, bad reports about 'this punk group,' and people keep going on about the 'Black Horse.' Councillors are not happy, resident committees are not happy, the police had stormed in asking was it true that someone wanted to put a punk gig on, resurrect the Grey Topper! There's going to be an extraordinary meeting of the committee to see if they'll allow the gig to go ahead.

I want to be there to plead my case, but discover it's on a day I'll be in Manchester for the funeral of my sister's best friend Alison who's died of cancer too. So I prepare a letter for Enid to present to the committee. Maybe it's a wee bit sarcastic, but it's true what I say and guess they have already decided to cancel.

Dear All

    I'd like to address a few concerns that have arisen over the prospect of having the rock band the UK Subs play a gig in the village. It would be a shame if a few scaremongers (or is that squaremongers?) ruin what I'm sure would be a special night for many people and would raise money for Cancer Research UK.

    People are bandying the words 'Black Horse' about like it's the 'Black Death,' this is the middle ages and the plague is returning to the village. No one has mentioned the fact that the UK Subs – at the height of their fame as a Top 40 band in 1979, when punks ruled the day and everyone was young – played two memorable gigs in the village at the Grey Topper without any trouble flaring up.

    The infamous incident at the Black Horse was many years ago and was not triggered off by any incitement from the band. It was caused by a few mindless young National Front skinheads from Heanor. Who would NOT be at any UK Subs in Jacksdale even though they'd be grown up men by now.

    Punk is now 30 years old. I went, with a couple of the one time Topper punks (Nige Cockayne and Tink), to see the well-known Irish band Stiff Little Fingers on their '30th anniversary tour' in Derby last year. The audience wasn't full of young spiky tops, carrying bike chains and sniffing glue (that was a false stereotypical image of punk 30 years ago anyway), no it was full of bald heads and beer bellies, many a grandad too I'd guess.

    The UK Subs have never been a group known for violence at their gigs and have never been banned from any venue (other than the Black Horse). Lead singer Charlie Harper is now in his 60's, his group a professional rock 'n' roll band that tour all over the world. (this is NOT the Sex Pistols in 1977 I'm trying to book here). I think it's time to mention him.

    Of all the bands that I've contacted, that once played the Grey Topper, Charlie Harper has been the most helpful. His band have recently toured America, Japan and Australia, Europe to come, they don't need to play Jacksdale but have agreed to because of the Grey Topper and he likes the idea of what I'm doing.

    This gig would be the last chapter in the Grey Topper story. Something to capture the old spirit of the village, when Jacksdale was famous for having one of the best music venue's in the East Midlands. Other bands that played the Grey Topper have also shown interest in

coming back here for a gig too if the UK Subs gig goes ahead and goes
well, which I've no doubt it would given the chance.

    Yours sincerely
    Tony Hill

On the way from Alison's funeral to her wake I get the call from the Welfare on my mobile.

'It's not gone at all well Tony I'm afraid,' Enid starts.

She's doesn't need to say any more, I just thank her for her support knowing she wanted it on and for being the voice of reason. 'It would have been good for us,' she says.

I say I hope the committee have a happy time continuing to live their *Life On Mars* in 1973.

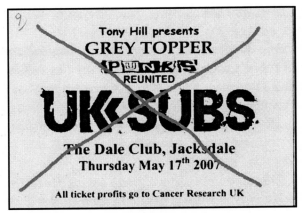

Cancelled.

Two days after the Welfare cancel, it's Easter Monday, from my kitchen – from everywhere in my home in fact – I can hear loud music booming out. At first I thought it was from the car stereo of some youths parked up on my street. But it continues and - as I leave my house to walk to a pub in Westwood - I realise it's coming from the Welfare. They've got a DJ set up outside, who's currently blasting out the Beastie Boys 'Fight for Your Right to Party.' How fucking ironic I'm thinking as this is playing as I pass by.

'Lets PARRRDDDY,' The DJ shouts into his mike. His posse

– all four of them – give it large by looking forlornly into the distance whilst supping their pints of mild and best.

Sound waves were causing hanging baskets to sway dangerously. Topper punk Feff, who lives across the road, reckons it was so loud his windows rattled.

'There's no place in village for racket like that yowf, it should be pulled dahn,' I tell him.

I'm really determined to get the gig on somewhere now and show those ignorant feckers how wrong they were, even though there is now only just over a month to go. Junktion 7 are still up for it, but they can't fit it in on the 17th at this short notice. Then I think about the MFN club, 'the place to be for bikers and petrol heads'. It's only about 5 miles away, outside of Eastwood. The choice word there being 'outside.' Yeah the name MFN stands for 'Middle of Fucking Nowhere,' so no moaning residents, committees or snooping councillors surely?

The drawbacks I see with MFN are 1. It's owned and run (with his son Lee) by Malcolm Allured, ex drummer with Showaddywaddy! One of the groups that were blown out of the water when punk came along, so how would he feel about putting on a gig for that scene? 2. MFN is only a few miles from Heanor and BNP central where the skinheads that sparked the riot at the 'Black Horse' (see I can't stop saying it now) came from. Oh what the fuck, at this stage I'll take the risk.

I ring to arrange a meeting with Malcolm Allured and his son Lee at MFN. It's a gorgeous sunny evening when I go up there, I feel a bit of a twat in my little Corsa as it's bikers night and the sun has bought them out in their hundreds, looking cool as fuck they're all swerving around me on the meandering country road you have to go along to get to the Middle of Fucking Nowhere. I have support tonight though, a lot of my friends are bikers and two of them Feff and Gary said they'll meet me up there.

I'm admiring the collection of Showaddywaddy silver, gold

and platinum discs, plus other press cuttings on the wall of the bar when Malcolm comes over. It's daft, I sort of pictured him in 1970's get up, pink suit, flares, shades and a medallion. When in actual fact he just looks like a seasoned, cool old rock dude, an old punk in fact, grey short hair, goatee beard, black t-shirt, combat trousers and boots.

He seems jovial enough (guess he would be with this unseasonable April sunshine bringing out all these bikers so early in the season) as he shakes my hand. His son Lee soon joins us. They're both rushed off their feet they tell me, so I put my gig proposal to them quick as.

The 17th is free they tell me and they've no problem putting it on, they'll even print the tickets for me. At first I think the room hire fee is a bit steep but when they take me into see the venue itself – where the night's group are sound checking - I'm very impressed. It's like a small Rock City, and the price includes a proper sound engineer, bar staff and security. We shake on the booking and Lee suggests I come back up the following day, around teatime, when it's quieter, to discuss things further.

When I do I find a gate closed, blocking vehicle access, so park up by the canal and walk over to MFN, everything is locked up so I bang on the door. Two fierce looking Dobermans bark at me from the top of a flat roof. Moments later Lee pops his head out of a window and says he'll be down shortly. I sit on a bench at an outside table, then spot the dogs coming down the steps in my direction, I'm about to leg it and jump in the canal having been bitten – on the arse – in a pub before.

'Don't mind them,' says Malcolm following them.

The Dobermans trot over and I nervously pat them on the head. It's not them that's biting today though.

'What you doing here I thought we shook on it last night?' Says Malcolm tetchily.

'Lee told me to come up now, I've brought some posters,' I reply nodding to the ones rolled up in my hand.

'Oh.'

It's another glorious spring night, MFN may be the middle of fucking nowhere for business but it's a lovely location, a river, canal and meadows, especially on a day like this.

'This is the life,' I comment with nothing better to say.

'Is it? Is it?' Says Malc grumpily shaking his head. 'How much does this punk group usually charge?' He enquires.

I tell him the price, which is a reduced fee that the Subs are doing it for.

'Huh! I was making £10,000 a night with my version of Showaddywaddy a few years back,' he replies with a note of triumph in his voice. 'Until the bastards took me to court and put a stop to it.'

I not sure if he's talking about the rest of the original Showaddywaddy and don't want to pry with the grouchy mood he's in. There is something kinda funny about him when in a mood though, you're not quite sure when he's taking the mickey, which I like. I'd be disappointed if an old rocker had been any other way.

Lee's with us by now and, as Malc skulks off to walk the dogs, he turns to me and tells me the reason for his bad mood.

'Don't mind him, he's got it on him today, he's got to go to court, again, tomorrow.'

What he tells me I know all to well by now, it's like reading about Alf's never ending struggle to keep the Topper open in the 1970's. Problems with a handful of residents spoiling it for everyone else, problems with councils, music licences, the police. Noise abatement notices have not only been served because of noise from car rallies and bikes and music, but there's even complaints if they put on a firework display.

It's all too familiar and I've now a lot of sympathy for Malc, who's poured nearly a million pounds into the place. It's even worse now than in Alf's day, I'm pretty certain that if he had been born at a later time and came up with the idea of opening the Grey Topper in Jacksdale, in this day and age it wouldn't get

169

past the planning phase at the local council.

Lee also tells me that, in the cold light of day, that they have a few concerns about the gig – oh feck here we go, who's mentioned the 'Black Horse?' - am I sure that I can get this gig on and get enough people to turn up in the short space of time I now have?

I'm not, but there's no way I'm going to give up now.

'We'll put it on, no problem, we just don't want you to be out of pocket, we've had this before, you can't get people to come out here for gigs.'

'They'll come out of the woodwork for the UK Subs,' I assure him, not sure if they will, 'I'll get something in the local papers,' I continue, not sure that I will.

'Ok, we'll print the tickets and get the posters up ASAP.'

I drive away relived, I trust these people to stick to their word.

Topper punk Feff is now helping me with putting the gig on, we've got to come up with a quick fire plan of action, we're discussing this and possible support bands in his front room when this young woman with shocking pink hair passes by the window. She's an alternative Avon Lady. As she pushes the catalogue through the door, Feff shouts out jokingly.

'Take it back, there's no women here,' (he's recently split up from his girlfriend). Then opens the door to give it her back. I'm thinking 'she's got pink hair, she looks alternative, she might be into punk?' So I ask her if she wants to go to a gig and show her a flyer.

'Oh the UK Subs! Yeah I'd be up for that.'

Turns out she's just moved into the village. What's the chance of that happening? But several weeks later a similar thing happens. This time a young lad with a mohican comes to the door selling household items. Again I show him a flyer and he too says he'll come to the gig.

'Can't believe you've got the Subs to play around here,' he says impressed.

I feel obliged to buy a bag of dusters off him, but don't reckon it's a bad trade off.

Feff had given me the CD single of a potential support band from Derby, they're called Elvis Is Dead. They sound great -

'All hail the new kings of rock 'n' roll' - 'Like the Darkness, but for people who actually like metal' - 'Elvis is Dead is over the top, greasy rock and roll with more sleaze than a Spanish waiter in a strip club.'

I ring Rob the drummer and confirm I'd like them as a support. I'm starting to get a real buzz about trying to put a gig together, even the pressure, as my calendar shows far too few squares left to tick off to the day. I'm even getting a kick out of having to battle, beat and prove wrong the people who have tried to stop it (and want it all to end in chaos.)

I gather up a pile of tickets to take around to friends in the village to try and sell for me, after which I plan to go and watch my team Man United try and make a come back of their own (1-2 down in the European Cup), at a mates most probably, or might watch it with dad, he starts Chemo in 2 days time so maybe, fingers crossed, maybe he can make some sort of comeback as well.

I'm just about to leave the house, when mum calls in a panic. Can I take her and dad to the hospital, he's had a real bad day and looks terrible she tells me. I'm shocked when I pick them up, he's the worst he's been since being diagnosed with cancer, he looked fine just a few days before, out pottering about in his garden again. The jaundice has returned, he's in a lot of discomfort and at times doesn't even know where he is. This is very worrying. I feel we need to let my sister and brother know. But Elaine is on her way back from Nottingham and hasn't her mobile switched on and my brother Brian and wife Jo are on a holiday abroad.

We were told dad would be admitted straight onto a specialist cancer ward on his arrival at Notts City Hospital, but when we get there it's the same fucked up NHS story (thanks Tony Blair what difference you made?), they take him to emergency admissions, there is no bed and as dad has to sit scrunched up in pain on a flimsy chair, a stroppy nurse tells us it's the same for everyone and others were here before dad 'this woman here's been here 3 hours waiting to be seen,' she informs us.

It must be said, others are far nicer and when a doctor takes a quick look at dad - and his condition is faxed to them from our doctor - he is found a bed. I manage to contact Elaine and tell her it would be best if she gets down here. When she arrives a doctor takes us into his office and spells it out to us just how serious dad is, he has an infection that they are going to try and combat with antibiotics, but his body might no longer be strong enough to fight it, dad might not last the night.

I have to rush back to my car to top up the exorbitant parking fees in case I get clamped, on the way back I pass a ward where a television is on, Man Utd are winning 6-1. At dad's bedside I hold his hand and tell him this, as a way of saying 'come on dad United are making a comeback you can too.' His eyes widen 'six one,' he replies, and a smile appears on his face, he then tells me to take my sister and leave him with mum. He passes away shortly afterwards.

I'm devastated, we all are, even though we knew he was going to die it was still so sudden in the end. It's harder to deal with than I could have imagined. For the next week, until after dad's humanists funeral, I don't want to do anything, socialise, go out at all except to go and sit with mum and Elaine. I feel I must get this concert on now, but it's hard to pick myself up and do the hard sell to strangers.

The saints are coming, my mini Topper punk army are galvanised into action, ringing and calling around to see if there's anything they can do. They're like the one time riders of the punk apocalypse who've grown angel wings. None more than Feff, I've always had a lot of time for him, he took me under his wings when I was 16 and took me to gigs with his mates.

He's the most punk person I know, even though he's never had much money he's done the things he wanted to do, be it being a drummer in 80's cult Sheffield Goth band Ipso Facto supporting the likes of Death Cult (The Cult before they dropped Death) and Xmal Deutschland, or going down in a cage to face great white sharks or snowboarding (his current plans are to sell his house, move to Slovenia and start a business with his mate organising snowboarding holidays). Feff really gets the bit between his teeth, picking up flyers and heading off down the Nottingham punk and rock circuit every other night. Soon he's back with news he's got another support band lined up.

173

This lot are hardcore punks called Certified. A bit in the mould of 80's bands like Exploited. Listening to high-octane songs like 'Assassination City' on their MySpace site I know Feff's done a good job and they'll fit the bill too. Also they're connected to Foremans punk bar in the city and will bring a crowd from there with them.

So, while I wasn't up to facing people, I spent hours at home putting 'punk,' 'UK Subs' and the name of a local town into the MySpace search box to find people who might want to come to the gig. I've over 50 new punk friends in the space of a few days.

By the time I'm back on a mission to get the Grey Topper Punks Reunited gig on - that has now become very important for me for several reasons - there are only a few weeks to go. Even though me and Feff have drummed up a lot of interest for the gig in the very short space of time we've had, the tickets sales are actually only about 40.

With overheads around about £1000 and tickets costing £10, my target is, always has been, at least 100 sold. 150 is the crowd I'm hoping for. On advice, we have let it be known that there will be admission on the night, the Notts punk crowd are going to pay on the door.

I do interviews with two local papers *Nottingham Evening Post* and *The Ripley and Heanor*, who are both fascinated by the Grey Topper story and want to do bigger features at some point. A new shop in Eastwood called 'My Generation' selling scooter gear, rock t-shirts and memorabilia, takes a book of tickets off me and put posters up to help try and shift some for me. It may be all too late, can we really hope to get another 100 people to go to the Middle of Fucking Nowhere for a gig that everyone is singing Kaisers Chief's 'I Predict A Riot' about?

There is some timely free publicity of a sort, but I'm not sure if it's a good or bad thing. 'Warhead' by the UK Subs is on the soundtrack of cult Nottingham film director Shane Meadows latest film *This Is England*. Great, and it was filmed locally, good. And it's about a kid coming under the influence of the wrong type of skinhead, oh.

I'm cautiously optimistic the gig will go on now and to be honest really don't give a fuck if it does end in chaos, as long as it's on, even if we only sell 90 tickets I'll put up £200 of my own money to ensure the Topper punks have another good night and some money goes to Cancer Research UK. It's out of my control now. I had an idea that began to roll and now I can't stop it. It's like a snowball going down a steep valley side.

It could 1. Hit a rock, fall to pieces and be finished once and for all. 2. Turn into a huge snowball that people turn into a giant snowman that brings a smile to everyone who sees it or 3. Turn into an avalanche that causes chaos and destruction, the result of which people will chuck me into a deep, deep crevice.

With less than a week to go I'm disorganised, stressed out and not sleeping properly. I don't reckon I will sleep properly and relax until the night of the gig, after Charlie Harper has said his goodbyes to the crowd after the last encore and the money is in. The UK Subs rider - which includes a case of Carling and bottles of cider, is sat in my kitchen and I can't touch it! What kind of Taliban dreamt up torture is that? I crack and help myself to a few much-needed cans of lager, I'll make the numbers back up tomorrow.

There wasn't just alcohol in the rider, there were other essential items listed that Showaddywaddy Malc was none too impressed with when I read it out to him in the hope he'd get it in for me.

'Bottles of water, 6 still, 2 sparkling,' I said.

'That's really rock 'n' roll, you can sort that out,' he replied contemptuously.

'Two cartons of fruit juice.'

'Fucking fruit juice! Thought these were punks? Go on.'

'Tea and coffee on their arrival.'

'Get the fuck out of here.'

What I'm worrying about now is that Malc and Charlie are going to rub each other up the wrong way, and that the first trouble to kick off on the night will be a fight between the ageing drummer out of Showaddywaddy and a sixty-something punk rocker. Then am relieved to hear Malc will be on holiday that night and son Lee will be running the show.

With just a few days to go me and Feff ring Charlie to finalise things. Then I send him Mutlimap directions to MFN. He calls back just a wee bit concerned, saying he didn't realise where the gig was going to be and that it's 'a very dodgy area,' have I got security sorted as it's 'the most dangerous place we've ever played.' This, the comments from a band that have played just about every town in England and done gigs all over the world. 'There was this place called the Black Horse, all these National Front skinheads turned up, bloody football hooligans'…. Oh fuck, I break into their rider for a few cans of Carling.

Of course they're still coming, they're punk, Charlie's a great guy and I crossed my fingers behind my back as I gave him false words of assurance. I mean why should he be worried, why should I be stressed, the gig is only taking place on the Notts/Derbyshire boarder, no rivalry there, old style and hardcore spiky tops are coming from inner-city Nottingham to mix it in the mosh pit with Derby and Ilkeston punks and skinheads from Heanor, no there's no rivalry there at all….praise be to Allah…I broke into the UK Subs rider for a few cans of Carling.

On Monday I heard that our main support act Elvis Is Dead were to split, at first I thought bollocks! Elvis Is Dead is dead! But thankfully they're playing all gigs already booked until June…I broke into UK Subs rider for a few cans of Carling.

I've spent hours and hours listening to piles of borrowed punk CD's so I can burn about 3 hours worth to be played by the DJ (I'm basically paying this lad to insert a CD and press play every so often) before and in-between groups. Most of the old school punk stuff is great, but I was given this very dodgy hardcore post punk compilation, 10 CD's, everything recorded live, badly, in all about 50 feckin hours worth and everything on them was shit, I was close to a nervous breakdown at the end....I broke into UK Subs rider for a few bottles of cider.

This post punk stuff was supposed to make the followers of hardcore band Certified happy, but I decided to fuck it, it's the Topper punks night, so old school classic stuff it is. Well apart from 'White Riot,' and 'Smash It Up' which might be a touch incendiary.

The venue sound engineer Barney was a bit worried about fitting the groups in on schedule because of 'changeovers,' 'backlines' and other technical shite I don't understand. I've not told him yet that we've added another band to the bill. They're called S-PUNK. Their bassist Jason runs Foremans punk bar in Nottingham, he got in touch wishing to play as his mum has terminal cancer. I'm chasing ticket cash up all over the place.....I go and break into UK Subs rider for some more ale, I'll replenish it tomorrow, the day - devil willing - the Grey Topper Punks Reunited concert is finally to take place.

When I get up in the morning the first thing I do is turn on my computer to see if I have any messages on hotmail or MySpace. It's on the latter that I come across the following messages on Certified's site.

'Good to see you chaps last night. Pity you didn't get to play, hope Shauns ok? See ya soon. ACAB.'

'Alrite lads, fuckin shame bout last night, it put a downer on the whole gig I thought. I hope the kickin the filth gave Shaun was enough and they don't charge him, but knowin how they operate they'll probably screw him, cunts. See yous soon. Trav and the nags.'

Shaun's the lead singer. Shit! What's gone off now? I haven't a contact number for them, Feff has but he's at work until 2.30 p.m. I ring Charlie around then to see if they're on the way.

'Not yet, the drivers not shown up yet, might have to come on the train.'

'The train! The nearest station's miles away, what about

your instruments and stuff?'

'Only joking, we should be on the road in about 20 minutes.'

'Oh, nice one Charlie.'

Setting off from London around 3.00 pm? To get here for the sound check at 6.00 pm? It's still pushing it I'm thinking. But what the fuck do I know, I'm talking to a guy who's played thousands of gigs over the last 30 years.

I go up town to collect the ticket money in from My Generation, then get more cash out of the bank so I've enough on me to pay the band and overheads in case enough isn't taken on the door. Then I go to Morrisons to put the UK Subs rider back together, before taking it down to MFN, I'm still missing something off the list though, 4 towels. It's 4.45 p.m. the shops will be closing soon, so I hurry along Eastwood high street to find a place that might sell them. Ah the trusty CO-OP home store. All they have of the right size and price though, are purple ones covered in swirl designs. Feck, I can't give them to a punk band I was thinking, luckily they found some plain blue ones in the back.

Feff has some good news, Certified can make it. I drop my car off back in Jacksdale, meet up with Feff, and another mate Gary gives us a lift up MFN about 5.30 p.m. So we wait for the UK Subs arrival....and wait....and wait, Elvis Is Dead are here, Certified and S-Punk and their multi coloured entourage pile in, but no one can sound check until after the Subs. It's 6.45 p.m. – the doors open in 45 minutes and they still haven't showed. Feff goes and gives them a call, I hit the bar.

'They're still in Long Eaton, they must have come off the M1 at the wrong junction.'

Long Eaton is over 10 miles away and it's another 30 minutes before I hear the words I'd longed to hear.

'The Subs are here,' Feff informs me, prising me from the bar.

Charlie greets me warmly. I'm immediately envious of his thick, spiky bleached blond and black spiky hair. He's with his beautiful young Japanese wife Yuko as well.

'Hi Tony, thought we'd never find the place its in the middle of fucking nowhere.'

'Funny you should say, that's what MFN means,' I laugh. 'How did you ever find Jacksdale? In the Grey Topper day's that was BFB?'

'What's that?'

'Back of Fucking Beyond.'

'We found it to that Sun Inn in Eastwood like you said, then were lost, luckily we spotted this punk coming out of Morrisons with a whisky bottle in his hand and guessed he'd be coming here so asked him (this is Mansfield Punk you've not heard the last of him). It's alright down here, just passed a mill pond wish I had my fishing rod with me.'

Charlie goes off to do the soundcheck and asks me if I'll help Yuko find a place where she can sell their merchandise, which I don't mind at all! She tells me how well the Subs first tour of Japan, Australia and New Zealand had gone (this is the first gig since their return).

Sound engineer Barney gets all the bands through the soundcheck in about 20 minutes, this is punk after all. The doors open and punka's old and new, plus a scattering of skinheads, start to pour in. I'm starting to get a real buzz of excitement now, and, by the time the first support act Elvis Is Dead have taken to the stage, I hear that enough are already in to have cleared my overheads. I can at last relax and enjoy the occasion.

Despite the fact that Elvis Is Dead are to split soon, they give it their all and end with a storming cover of the Anti Nowhere League's 'So What.'

'Have a good night we were Elvis is dead, so fucking what.' Yells the singer into the mike giving an indication of the tension in the band.

Perhaps Elvis Is Dead verge on the side of metal too much for this crowd of mainly old school punks as no one was really down the front for them, except mohican topped 'Mansfield

Punk' which was painted on the back of his leather jacket below a *Never Mind The Bollocks here's the Sex Pistols* painting.

Next up are brilliant punk covers band S-PUNK, sounds of Topper 79 fill MFN - Sex Pistols 'Bodies' brings bodies into the mosh pit and friends for Mansfield Punk, who after taking another huge gulp from his pint, bounces off them like a demented Weeble.

One thing I'm already picking up on is the atmosphere, it's great, not a sniff of trouble or anyone sniffing glue as committee members and others envisaged there would be. It's a weird, wonderful feeling to have created this and see it all come together and people having a good time. Has the evil spirit of the 'Black Horse' been exorcised? Only the UK Subs can do that and more are coming in so better not count me rock chicks yet. Next on stage are confrontational hardcore band Certified as well.

No fear, they rip through a blistering set of 3-minute protest and ant-establishment songs, the energy of which even gets pogos of approval from the old school punk Topper crowd.

Oh fuck yes! Nottingham punk legend - and lead singer of Sic Boy Federation - Hendrix Dead Boy is in the house! I can't get a better seal of approval than that.

The moment I've been dreaming of for 8 months is drawing near, but before the UK Subs take to the stage Barry from Cancer Research UK (who lost his wife in December and has given up his own time - with colleague Pat - to walk around with collection buckets) asks me if he can say something over the tannoy. I take him to the mixing booth where Barney hands him a mike and turns down the X-Ray Spex. Barry delivers a poignant little speech and thanks everyone.

'Together we will beat cancer,' he says last off to applause.

It being a loud punk concert, with predictions of violence, I had been worried about Barry coming along as he's in his 70's. But he'll say to me later 'It's not really my scene but I was pleasantly surprised' (and there's over £100 in the buckets alone).

His speech pulled at the three chords of my punk heart and made me think of dad, I have five minutes out, in the toilet on my own. I like to think of him up there watching it all with the Topper owner Alf, both moaning about the music still but agreeing we're not a bad bunch really.

The UK Subs take to the stage to loud cheers, looking around at the size of the crowd I reckon I've reached my target. I'm well satisfied in the time we've had to get it on here. They're a minute into 'CID' when Mansfield Punk staggers on stage, trips over cables and brings things to a halt for several anxious minutes. Japanese guitarist Jet has been unplugged.

'That's Japanese technology for you,' jokes Charlie.

Thankfully all connections are restored, 'Live In A Car' reverberates around the room, Mansfield Punk is climbing up on the stage again, Topper punk Spike – all 17 stone of him – puts a persuasive arm around him and leads him down the steps at the side of the stage, but Mansfield Punk slips down half of them and is it out cold. He's not been pushed or banged his head, he's hammered as Charlie observes.

'He's had Morrisons deal of the day buy one bottle of Whisky get one free.'

Security has to roll Mansfield Punk out of the emergency exit at the side of where he's snoring away.

Charlie's Subs may have an ever-changing line-up but they sound as great as 1979 as they tear through 'New York Sate,' 'Tomorrows Girls' and 'Teenage.' After this Charlie pauses and says into the mike.

'A big thank you for Tony, where is he? Alright mate, I drove through a mill to get here, he's been through the mill to get this on…this is for all you Topper punks.'

The intro to 'Warhead' booms out, Topper punks pat me on the back, hug me even, before pogoing to the Subs classic. Then they try to strangle me, in an affectionate kind of way, as the Subs play another Top 40 song that evokes memories of Topper

79 'Stranglehold,' I'm so exhausted and pissed I nearly pass out, good way to go though.

'You pulled it off,' shouts Royal Oak landlord Byrnie big smile on his face.

After the encore I realise I've still got to pay the Subs and want to check how much money is in. Lee takes me into the office and informs me that the first wad - from door takings - is for the hire of the venue, but there is another, I'm defiantly in profit. Only trouble is, what with the other ticket money I've collected in, plus money I'd withdrawn from the bank, I have money stashed in every pocket. So go and lock myself in a toilet cubicle, kneel on the floor and try and count the right amount out for the Subs, which wasn't very easy in the state I was in. There's hundreds left over for Cancer Research UK 'Where did it all go wrong,' I laugh to myself.

Me and Feff spend a happy hour chatting to Charlie back stage as the rest of the Subs load up their gear. At one point this man bursts into the room. It's about 12.45 a.m.

'Where's Charlie, where's Charlie?' he says excitedly.

Although not from Jacksdale, he's a one-time Topper punk who's driven all the way back from London (where he's working) at 90 mph to get here for the gig.

'Sorry you missed it,' Charlie tells him. 'It was a great gig, ten times better than I expected, which was a tiny back room with our own toilet and baying load of skinheads.'

'Be gone Black Horse, be gone!' I shout inside my head.

After a few hours back stage sharing a few beers and chatting to Charlie, me and Feff set off to walk the 5 or so miles to Jacksdale about 2.00 a.m. I'm pissed and happy, the stars are shining above, there's some spinning around my head too.

We're walking along the country road from MFN, this runs adjacent to the A610 by-pass. I look into its wooded embankment and there is Mansfield Punk slumped against a tree. I point him out to Feff and we climb over the barrier.

'Are you alright mate?' We ask.

182

'Er…where the fuck…am I?'

'Next to a bypass in Eastwood, you've been to a gig remember?'

He gives a bleary eyed nod of recall, like it all happened 30 years ago and he's just woken from a dream. 'Yeah fuckin excellent.'

We help him to his feet and lead him up to the town centre, plonk him down on a seat outside of Morrisons and order him a taxi.

As we're walking away he shouts -

'Punk lives!'

'Yeah and the Grey Topper,' I call back.

◆ **PUNK** is alive and well — and these days it seems to have a heart of gold. To celebrate the punk days at the old **Grey Topper Club** at **Jacksdale**, sadly now nothing more than a memory, ex-regular **Tony Hill** organised a reunion gig, held at the MFN at Shipley. He rounded up top band UK Subs, pulled in support from **Elvis Is Dead**, **Certified** and **S-Punk** … and between them they raised £550 for **Cancer Research**.

Nottingham Evening Post: 'Ex-regular,' wish I had been.

'Do Anything You Wanna Do' – Eddie & The Hot Rods.

The Hot Rods played the Topper too (when called Buckshee) as you'll now see by moving on to the Grey Topper A-Z.

GREY TOPPER
A-Z

Then – After – Now

Here I've tried to list as many acts as possible (plus things and people of interest) that appeared at the Grey Topper between 1969 and 1981. I've not added a full discography for the bands/singers, just the records of relevance or that indicates the success they achieved. When these appear in the description the chart position is in brackets. MT = Many Times.

	Group	Date	Chart Pos
	Academy	6 Sep 74	

Adam and the Ants

Then	Punk band formed by Stuart Goddard (Adam Ant) in 1977. Other band members were – Matthew Ashman (guitar/vocals), Dave Barbe (drums), Andy Warren (bass/vocals). They arrived in Jacksdale in the middle of the 'Zerox' tour.		
GT Gig		29 Jul 79	
Record	Young Parisians	Oct 78	-
	Zerox	Jul 79	-
After	Dave Barbe and Matthew Ashman left to form Bow Bow Wow. Andy Warren joined the Monochrome Set. Adam and his new Ants became *King's of the Wild Frontier*, superstardom, teen adulation and many No.1's beckoned.		
Record	King's of the Wild Frontier	21 Feb 81	2
	Stand and Deliver	9 May 81	1
	Prince Charming	12 Sep 81	1
	Goody Two Shoes	22 May 82	1
Now	After the hits began to subside Adam Ant moved to LA and became and actor, gaining many roles on TV and in film. Out of the limelight, suffering from manic depression, he was charged with threatening members of the public with an imitation firearm in 2002. Later he bravely		

appeared in a documentary *The Madness of Prince Charming* to discuss his illness.

Matthew Ashman died from diabetes complications in 1995 aged 35.

Affro   1 Aug 74

Angelic Upstarts
Socialist, anti-fascist punk band from the Northeast. Formed by singer 'Mensi' Mensworth and guitarist Ray Cowie after being inspired by The Clash on the 'White Riot' tour. The Angelic Upstarts were one of the first 'Oi' bands.

GT gig   2 Sep 79

Record   I'm An Upstart   21 Apr 79   31
           Teenage Warning   11 Aug 79   29

After/now Mensi has fronted various line-ups of the Angelic Upstarts.

The **Applejacks**
1960's beat group from Birmingham best known for their Top 10 hit 'Tell Me When,' and The Beatles cover 'Like Dreamers Do.'

GT gig   30 Nov 75

The **Art Movement**
Late 1960's English pop band that became the backing band for Roy Orbison.

GT gig   28 Jun 69

Aztec   7 Dec 75

B-Movie
Post-punk, 'New Romantic' band from Mansfield, Notts. Toured with Duran Duran. Did several Radio 1 sessions and featured on the *Some Bizarre* album - a showcase for up

and coming acts like Depeche Mode, The The, Soft Cell and Blancmange.

B-Movie split in 1982, but singer Steve Hovington and guitarist Paul Statham reformed the band in 2006 for a series of dates.

GT gig		5 Apr 80	
Record	Remembrance Day	18 Apr 81	61
	Nowhere Girl	27 Mar 82	67

Babe Ruth

Progressive rock band from Hertfordshire with lead singer, Janita Haan. Had more success in North America (their 'First Base' went gold in Canada). On guitar was Bernie Marsden who went on to join Whitesnake.

GT gig   22 Feb 77

Baby Dolls   15 Apr 77

Band Called O

Rock band, did four sessions for John Peel between 1974 -77.

GT gig   24 Jun   75

Band Of Heroes

GT gig   13 Aug 77

1 Jun   78

Band Of Joy

Rock band from Birmingham. The original 1960's line up is famous for having included future Led Zeppelin members John Bonham and Robert Plant, plus the Slade's Noddy Holder was their roadie.

This version of the band was reformed by Kevin 'Carlisle Egypt' Gammond (guitar/vocals), Paul Lockey (bass) after Plant and Bonham went on to start a slightly bigger project. Band Of Joy played the Grey Topper, Jacksdale in spring 1979 to a few hundred people. A few months later Led

Zeppelin did two nights at the Knebworth festival to an audience of over 100,000.

GT gig   11 Mar 79

Bandylegs (see Quartz)   29 Aug 76

JJ Barnes
US Soul artist who started his career sharing the bill with Aretha Franklin and The Miracles, signed up by Motown for his song writing abilities. Hugely popular with the UK Northern Soul scene in the 1970's.

GT Gig   14 Apr 74

Bay City Rollers
Then   Scottish, poptastic, white flared, tartan-adorned band.

GT gig   13 Jan   74
                                                10 Mar 74

Record   Keep On Dancing   18 Sep 71   9
            Remember (Sha-La-La)   9 Feb   74   6

After   'Rollermania' swept the country as they became the most screamed at group since the Beatles.

Record   Shang-A-Lang   27 Apr 74   2
            Summerlove Sensation   27 Jul   74   3
            All Of Me Loves All Of You 12 Oct 74   4
            Bye Bye Baby   8 Mar 75   1
            Give A Little Love   12 Jul   75   1

Now   After selling over 70 million records they fragmented into several Roller groups. Lead singer Les Mckeown's being the most popular and still tour today.

BC's   27 Aug 74

Beano   14 Aug 77

Beautiful Day   13 Aug 76

Beaver   25 Mar 74

Dave **Berry**
Charismatic 1960's pop idol from Sheffield. Had many hits including 'The Crying Game,' 'Mama' and 'Little Thing's. The Sex Pistols did a cover of his song 'Don't Gimme No Lip Child' and acknowledged him as an inspiration.

GT gig	2 Jul	70	
	9 Feb	75	

Bethnal
New Wave band influenced by The Who. Released two albums *Dangerous Times* and *Crash Landing* (made with the help of Pete Townsend). Appeared on *The Old Grey Whistle Test* but failed to fulfil the potential of their live performances. Split in 1980. All members of the group continued to work in the music industry.

GT gig   24 Jul 77

Biffo   21 Jun 74

Bill Haley and the Comets
Rock 'n' roll great and the first to make the form of music popular to the masses in the 1950's.

GT gig   5 Apr 74

Record	Shake Rattle and Roll	17 Dec 54	4
	Rock Around The Clock	14 Oct 55	1
	See You Later Alligator	9 Mar 56	7

After   Continued to tour until shortly before his death from a brain tumour in 1981.

Bite   29 Nov 74

Bitter Suite/The Phil Brodie Band
Rock and blues touring musicians that were almost house bands at the Grey Topper.

Blackfoot Sue

Stomping rock group from Birmingham whose members were – Tom Farmer (lead vocals, bass), twin brother David Farmer (drums, vocals), Eddie Golga (lead guitar, vocals), Alan Jones (guitar, vocals). They played the Grey Topper many times in the mid 1970's, often with busloads of their followers in tow. Still on the road today.

Record	Standing In The Road	12 Aug 72	4
	Sing Don't Speak	16 Dec 72	36

Bluebird   MT

Brandysnap   17 Jul 76

Brothers

One hit wonders pop band.

GT gig		13 Mar 77
Record	Sing Me	29 Jan 77	8

Buckshee

Young band from Southend, playing stripped back rock 'n' roll.

GT gig   28 Sep 74

After   Changed their name to Eddie and the Hot Rods and became one of the main bands on the London pub rock circuit. In Feb 1976 they played the Marquee and were supported by a young band called the Sex Pistols, who trashed their equipment.
In 1977 their single 'Do Anything You Wanna Do' went Top 10 and became a punk anthem.

Buddy And The Dimes   6 Jun 76

Bumper   5 Aug 76

Burgundy   9 Sep 77

Burlesque
Cult 'art-rock' band that skirted the London pub rock and
punk rock scenes ('but were definitely neither') co-led by
Billy Jenkins and Ian Trimmer.

GT gig   4 Sep 74

Billy **Campbell And The Mighty Sparrows**
GT gig   13 Feb 70

Candlewick Green
Comedy band, appeared on TV talent show *Opportunity
Knocks* for nine consecutive weeks.

GT gig   12 Oct 75

Record   Who Do You Think -
           - You Are   23 Feb 74   21

Candy Choir
Beach Boys, west coast influenced band. As well as doing
their own gigs they toured and recorded as the backing
band for Chrispian St. Peters, Johnny Kidd and Barry
Ryan.

GT gig   20 Sep 69
                                         31 Jan 70

Capricorn   24 Aug 74

Carl's Fables
Local 'bad boy' rock band from Ilkeston with a lead singer
who was 'a cross between Joe Cocker, with the
mannerisms of Jethro Tull's Ian Anderson.' Their
performance ended with Carl breaking a red ink capsule in
his mouth. Finally, with 'blood' streaming out of the
corners of his mouth onto his chest under strobe lighting,
there would be a blinding flash and explosion. The
audience were left momentarily blinded, and upon

recovering their sight a few seconds later they'd find the stage empty.

GT gig	30 Mar 70

Cash MT

Castle 9 May 77

The **Casuals**
Pop group who had two Top 40 hits in 1968 – 'Jesamine' (2) and 'Toy' (30)

GT gig	10 Apr 77

Cathedral 6 Mar 71

Chatterley Mews 22 Nov 74

Chimera
Then Acid-folk, psychedelic band fronted by two young women Francesca Garnett and Lisa Bankoff. They recorded an album produced by Pink Floyd's Nick Mason and featured Fleetwood Mac's Bob Weston on guitar.

GT gig	18 Oct 69

After Chimera's album wasn't released until 2002 (on vinyl, 2006 on CD) and is now looked on as a 'lost masterpiece' in acid-fold, pyschedelia circles. The enclosed booklet tells of the bands adventures in swinging London. Francesca Garnett and Lisa Bankoff also wrote a book *Making It: Famous Names And Silly Girls.*

Chrome Molly
NWOBHM from Leicester. Later supported Alice Cooper and Ozzy Osbourne. Did a version of Squeeze's single 'Take Me I'm Yours' (with Jools Holland on piano).

GT gig	30 Aug 79

Cisco (LG) MT

Jimmy **Cliff**

Jamaican reggae superstar, contemporary of Bob Marley and Desmond Dekker. Starred in the cult 1970's film *The Harder They Come* for which his songs – 'You Can Get It If You Really Want,' 'Many Rivers To Cross,' 'The Harder They Come' and 'Pressure Drop' - were the inspiration for and provided the soundtrack.

GT gig		19 May	74	
Record	Wonderful World -			
	- Beautiful People	25 Oct	69	6
	Vietnam	28 Feb	70	46
	Wild World	8 Aug	70	8
	Clockwork Orange	29 Aug	74	
	Clockwork Toys	23 Jan	71	
	Colours Of Love	30 Jan	70	
	Copper Kettle	11 Apr	74	
	Cottage	2 Nov	74	

The **Count Bishops**

Powerful pub rock and blues band championed by *NME*'s Charles Sharr Murray. Toured with Motorhead. When they came to the Grey Topper they were still getting over the loss of guitarist and songwriter Zenon De Fleur who had died in hospital in March, a week after a car accident. This was just after the completion of their third album *Cross Cuts*. The band drafted in a stand-in guitarist and carried on with the tour to promote the album, but split at the end of the year.

A young Jools Holland played piano on the album.

GT gig	20 May 79

Crazy Cavan
Teddy Boy band with their own unique 'crazy rhythm' sound. Credited with inspiring the rockabilly revival and groups like psychobilly kings The Meteors.

GT gig   17 Dec 77

The **Crickets**
Backing band of rock 'n' roll legend Buddy Holly.

GT gig   30 Jun 74

The **Crystals**
1960's US girl group. One of the first to be produced by the legendary Phil Spector.

GT gig   28 Apr 74

Record			
He's A Rebel	22 Nov 62	19
Da Doo Ron Ron	20 Jun 63	5
Then He Kissed Me	19 Sep 63	2
I Wonder	5 Mar 64	36

Curley   MT

Cyanide
Then   Punk band from York, released the singles 'Mac The Flash,' 'Fireball' and 'I'm A Boy.'

GT gig   9 May 79

After   A compilation of Cyanide's material was released in 2000 *The Punk Rock Collection*. Lead singer Bob DeVries died of natural causes in his flat in York in 2005.

■

Danta   27 Jan 74

Dafne And The Tenderspots
Then   New Wave band that included Dafne Nancholas on vocals and Alan Wilder a.k.a. Alan Normal on keyboard.

GT gig		19 May 79	

After Alan Wilder dropped the 'Normal' and joined New Romantic superstars Depeche Mode.

Dafne and her partner Graham Smith created 'Calmtime' that 'blends music and natural sounds with the lullaby effect – the intimate sound of melodic humming - and warm, gentle music to create an atmosphere of calm and comfort that anyone can use.' Mainly listened to by mothers and their babies.

Darts

Nine piece, novelty doo-wop revivalists, formed by 'mad, bulging-eyed bass singer' Den Hegarty. They had five Top 10 hits in the late 70's.

GT gig		23 Oct 77	
Record	Daddy Cool	5 Nov 77	6

After Den Hegarty left the band after a dispute with management in 1979 and landed a job on classic, anarchic kids TV show *TISWAS* shouting 'BONG!' and - to the envy of the nations adolescent boys and their dads - rolling about in custard with Sally James. He had a stint as a cable TV show quizmaster, now he's a psychologist.

Dateline 3 Apr 76

Dead End Kids

One hit wonders with a version of The Honeycombs 'Have I The Right.' They did get to perform it on *TISWAS* though, and the Grey Topper of course.

GT gig		7 May 77	
Record	Have I The Right	26 Mar 77	6

Desmond **Dekker**

Ska and reggae legend. His single 'Israelites' was the first reggae song to top the charts. This paved the way for other reggae acts like Bob Marley and Jimmy Cliff who played the Grey Topper the same weekend as Dekker. His music was also an influence on the punk bands that incorporated elements of reggae into their music and the 2 Tone Ska /mod revival. Dekker died of a heart attack in May 2006.

GT gig		18 May 74	
Record	007	12 Jul 67	14
	Israelites	19 Mar 69	1
	It Miek	25 Jun 69	7

Delegation
R&B/disco band formed by Jamaican Rick Bailey.

GT gig		19 Jun 77	
Record	Where Is The love	23 Apr 77	22
	You've Been Doing -		
	- Me Wrong	20 Aug 77	49

After   Although there was no more chart success in the UK, their single 'Oh Honey' was a huge hit in America reaching No.5 in the Billboard Charts. Rick Bailey's Delegation continues to record and tour. Rap artist Coolio had a huge hit by sampling 'Oh Honey.'

Detroit Emeralds
Soul group.

GT gig		26 Apr 74	
Record	Feel The Need In Me	10 Feb 73	4
	You Want It You Got It	5 May 73	12
	I Think Of You	11 Aug 73	27

Detroit Soul Machine   14 Mar 76

Doll By Doll
Then   Scottish New Wave band that fused blues, psychedelic, folk and punk. Fronted and formed by singer Jackie Leven, they released several well-received albums *Remember* and *Gypsy Blood* but never broke through to the mainstream.

GT gig   1 Apr 79

After	After Doll By Doll split in 1983 Jackie Leven set out on a solo career. After leaving a recording session for his first album he was the victim of a violent unprovoked attack in a North London street. Strangulation left him unable to speak or sing for nearly two years. Suffering from the psychiatric trauma from the attack his life spiralled down into heroin addiction.
Now	Jackie Leven beat his demons and addiction and is now an acclaimed folk singer. In 2005 he teamed up with best selling author Ian Rankin (*Rebus*) to make the album *Jackie Leven Said*. Rankin narrates a story and Leven provides the songs.

The **Drifters**

One of the longest running groups in pop history, with many line ups over the years (including Ben E King for a time) their music er drifted from Doo Wop, R&B, Gospel and Soul. Too many hits to list here, the most popular being 'Save The Last Dance For Me,' 'Under The Boardwalk,' 'Saturday Night At The Movies' and 'You're More Than A Number In My Little Red Book.' Referred to Jacksdale as 'Jacksonville.'

Eastwood	MT

Duane **Eddy**

Rock 'n' roll 'twangy' guitar hero. Had a huge number of Top 40 hits, the most famous being the theme tune to *Peter Gunn*.

GT gig	10 Aug 74

Edison Lighthouse

A group of session musicians gathered together to promote the single 'Love Grows (Where My Rosemary Goes)' written by producers Tony McCaulay and Barry Mason. It reached No.1 and sold 8 million copies worldwide.

| GT gig | 18 May 75 |

The **Elizabethans**

Then   Late 1960's beat influenced band formed by Chris Norman, (vocals/guitar/piano), Terry Uttley (bass/vocals) Alan Silson (lead guitar/vocals). Pete Spencer (drums) joined later.

| GT gig | 28 Feb 70 |

After   An infection affected Chris Norman's vocal chords, making his voice rougher in sound. The band became Smokie and had five Top 10 hits in the 70's, including 'Living Next Door Too Alice' (5). This track was re-released in 1995 as a duet with controversial northern comedian Roy Chubby Brown as 'Living Next Door To Alice (Who The F**k Is Alice)' and reached No.3.
Trivia; Smokie are also to blame for producing England football star Kevin Keegan's first single 'Head Over Heels In Love.'

Eric Bell Band

Eric Bell was a founding member of Irish rock band Thin Lizzy. He played guitar on their No.6 hit 'Whiskey In The Jar.' Left Thin Lizzy in 1973 and formed his own band.

| GT gig | 28 Jan 79 |

| **Eye To Eye** | 22 Oct 77 |

The **Exciters**

US soul band. After having a single 'Tell Him' in the charts in 1963, The Exciters returned with a Top 40 single 'Reaching For The Best' in 1975.

| GT gig | 20 Nov 76 |

| **Extasy** | 11 Sep 75 |

F

Fable	MT
Factotum	27 Jun 69
Family Affair	MT

Fashion

Then
Experimental New Wave band from Birmingham with 6ft 9′ tall lead singer/guitarist Luke James, John Mulliagan (bass/keyboards) and Dik Davies (drums). They released three singles and the album *Product Perfect* on their own 'Fashion Music' label but had little airplay on the radio.

GT gig   26 May 79

After
With a new singer, De Harris, Fashion had moderate success on the back of the New Romantic scene in 1982 with the singles 'Street Player' (46) and 'Love Shadow' (51) from the album *Fabrique*.
Original lead singer Luke James now sings the blues in the Bay Area of California.

Fischer-Z

Then
New Wave band formed by the enigmatic John Watts (vocal/ guitar). Had two minor hit singles in the UK but their albums sold over two million Worldwide.

GT gig   27 May 79

Record   The Worker   26 May 79   53
             Word Salad (album)   79

After
John Watts has resurrected Fischer-Z on several occasions and continues to work as an avant-garde solo artist. In 2006 he released the album *It Has To Be*, a collection of real life stories from people he met on travels around Europe turned into songs.

Fluff	MT
Follyfoot	MT

Wayne **Fontana**

Manchester born Glyn Ellis found fame with his name change and beat group Wayne Fontana And The Mindbenders in the mid 1960's with hits like 'Um Um Um Um Um Um' (5), 'Game Of Love' (2 in the UK, No.1 in the US) and as a solo artist 'Come On Home' (16) and 'Pamela Pamela' (11). Still performs on the nostalgia circuit.

GT gig   16 Oct   77

The **Foundations**

UK/West Indian soul group best known for their number one hit 'Baby Now That I've Found You,' and the Top 10 singles 'Build Me Up Butter Cup' (2), and 'In The Bad Bad Old Days.'

GT gig   25 May 75

Foxglove   21 Jun   79

                                          6 Sep   79

Freddie And The Dreamers

Zany 60's beat band from Manchester who had many hits including 'I'm Telling You Now' (2) and 'You Were Made For Me' (3).

GT gig   26 Nov 76

Frenzy   8 Aug 76

Raymond **Froggatt**

Birmingham singer/songwriter. A Topper favourite from the early/mid 1970's, 'Froggie' penned songs for The Dave Clark Five ('Red Balloon'), Cliff Richard, The Byrds and many more. Still tours today and has a huge following, many of which show up clutching cuddly toy frogs and waving green scarves.

GT gig   MT

Fumble

UK rock 'n' roll band that toured with Bill Haley, Chuck Berry, Fats Domino and David Bowie.

GT gig   MT

Billy Fury

Then   Liverpool born rock 'n' roll superstar. Had over 25 hits from 1959-1967. 'Halfway To Paradise' (3), 'Jealousy' (2), 'I'd Never Find Another You' (5), 'It's Only Make Believe' (10) are just some of the many.

GT gig   69 - 71

After   Needed open-heart surgery – a childhood illness had left it in a weak condition – in 1971, after which he retired from performing. Resurfaced in 1973 when he played rock 'n' roll singer Stormy Tempest in the film *That'll Be The Day* (starring David Essex).

Shortly after recording a comeback album Billy Fury collapsed and died in 1983, he was 43.

Gaffa

New Wave band from Nottingham, had a 'single of the week' in *NME*. Singer Wayne Evans and guitarist Clive Smith are now in a band called The Last Pedestrians.

GT gig   4 Mar 79

Geordie

Glam rock band from Newcastle. Their line up consisted of Brian Johnson (vocals), Vic Malcolm (guitar, vocals), Tom Hill (bass) and Brian Gibson (drums).

GT gig   26 May 74

Record   Don't Do That   2 Dec 72   32
          All Because Of You   17 Mar 73   6
          Can You Do It   16 Jun 73   13
          Electric Lady   25 Aug 73   32

| After | The band split in 1979. Brian Johnson became lead singer with heavy metal superstars AC/DC in 1980. |

Gerry And The Pacemakers
Merseybeat group who were the first band to reach No.1 in the charts with their first three singles – 'How Do You Do It,' 'I Like It' and 'You'll Never Walk Alone,' which became the anthem of the supporters of Liverpool Football Club.

| GT gig | 12 Nov 76 |

| **Gimik** | 6 Jul 78 |

| **Gingerbread** | 9 Jan 70 |

Girlschool
All female New Wave of British Heavy Metal (NWOBHM) band tinged with punk.

| GT gig | 1 Oct 78 |

| After | Signed a record deal, toured and recorded an EP with Motorhead, gained a cult following that they still play to today. |

| Record | St Valentine's Day -
- Massacre EP (with
Motorhead) | 2 Aug 80 | 5 |
| | Hit And Run (album) | 81 | 5 |

Gary Glitter

| Then | 'Godfather' of glam rock. Had 11 Top 10 hits including 'Rock And Roll' (2), 'Hello Hello I'm Back Again' (2) and 'I'm The Leader Of The Gang' (1). |

| GT gig | 72 - 73 |

| After/now | Was still a popular live performer until the discovery of child pornography on his computer in 1999. Left the country in shame, moved to Cambodia, chucked out, moved to Vietnam, jailed for child sexual abuse in 2005. |

The **Glitter Band**

Started out as the backing band for Gary Glitter, then had more success releasing their own singles.

GT gig		9 May 74	
Record	Angel Face	23 Mar 74	4
	Just For You	3 Aug 74	10
	Goodbye My Love	18 Jan 75	2

Glow 30 May 74

Grapevine 22 Jan 76

Great Expectations 8 May 76

No one else did, can't find anything about them.

Harmony Grass

Beach Boys influenced soft-rock band.

GT gig		28 Jun 70	
Record	Move In A Little Closer	29 Jan 69	24

Jet **Harris**

Former bass player with instrumental guitar heroes The Shadows. Also had three Top 5 hits after leaving the band and teaming up with Tony Meehan including No.1 single 'Diamond.'

GT gig 16 Apr 77

The **Headboys**

New Wave, power pop band.

GT gig		10 Jun 79	
Record	The Shape Of Things - - To Come	22 Sep 79	45

Head's Together 1 Feb 74

Hearts Of Soul		9 Mar 74	

Heatwave

Then   American servicemen brothers Johnny and Keith Wilder formed disco/funk band Heatwave whilst based in Germany in the mid 1970's. After several line ups they settled in Britain and teamed up with keyboard player and songwriter Rod Temperton (from Hull). Making up the rest of the band were American Jessie Whitten (guitar), Spaniard Mario Mantese (bass) and Czechoslovakian Ernest Berger (drums). Touring the Northern clubs brought them to Jacksdale, first in 1976.

GT gig		19 Dec 76	
Record	Boogie Nights	22 Jan 77	2
GT gig		27 Mar 77	
Record	Too Hot To Handle	7 May 77	15

After   Success in America, gold and platinum record sales followed before a series of tragedies struck. Jessie Whitten was stabbed to death near his parent's home in America. Mantese was severely injured in a car crash forcing him to leave the group. Songwriter Rod Temperton had already left by then, going on to write songs for Michael Jackson including the single 'Thriller.'

Heatwave reformed and continued to have hit singles until founder member and lead singer Johnny Wilder was also involved in a car accident leaving him paralysed from the neck down. This wasn't the end for the band, Wilder continued to produce and record vocals for them, as well as teaching students about the music industry until his dying in his sleep in May 2006 aged 56.

Hector
Glam rock group that adopted a 'Dennis the Menace styled image.'

GT gig   MT

Hello

North London glam rock band. Their debut album, *Keeps Us Off the Streets,* was released wrapped in a mock denim cover.

GT gig		26 Jan	75	
Record	Tell Him	9 Nov	74	6
	New York Groove	18 Oct	75	9

Helms Deep   5 Apr 75

Herman's Hermits with **Peter Noone**

Manchester pop band of the 1960's, part of the 'British Invasion' of the US. Sold more than 40 million records and some of their many hits included 'I'm Into Something Good,' 'Silhouettes,' 'No Milk Today,' and 'There's A Kind of Hush.'

GT gig   26 Oct 75

Highly Likely

The session band of Mike Hugg (Manfred Mann) who had a Top 40 hit with 'Whatever Happened To You,' the theme tune to classic 70's comedy series *Whatever Happened To The Likely Lads.*

GT gig   6 Jun 74

Highly Strung   14 Mar 75

High Q   28 Oct 75

Hobson's Choice   11 Sep 76

Honey Monster

A large, furry, yellow creature from the 'Sugar Puffs' TV commercials, where it worked alongside a young Kate Winslett making her acting debut and Henry McGee of Benny Hill fame. Released one single that failed to chart.

Left the music business shortly afterwards. Now runs a B&B in Clacton-On-Sea.

GT gig		27 Aug 77

Horizon	23 Jul 76

Hot Chocolate

Then Soul/disco band formed in Brixton, London. Fronted by the charismatic singer/songwriter Errol Brown.

GT gig		70 - 73	

Record	Love Is Life	15 Aug 70	6
	Brother Louie	14 Apr 73	7

After/now Hot Chocolate would have a hit every year from 1970-1984 (the only band to do so) including the classics 'You Sexy Thing' (2), 'So You Win Again' (1), 'It Started With A Kiss' (5) and 'Every 1's A Winner' (12) until they disbanded. They became hugely popular again in 1997 when 'You Sexy Thing' was used for the soundtrack to hit comedy film *The Full Monty*.

Errol Brown continues to perform as a solo singer and was awarded an MBE by the Queen in 2003. A year later he was presented with the Ivor Novello Award for 'outstanding contribution to popular music.'

Hotfoot Gale

Rockabilly band who had a single called 'Washin' Machine Boogie' (didn't chart).

GT gig		18 Feb 78

Hot Water

New Wave band from Bangor, Wales. Had two female lead singers - Sheila McCartney and Brenda Prescott. Caught the ear of Radio 1's John Peel and were booked for a session. Released a couple of singles 'Different Morning' and 'Get Lost!' before splitting. Their gig at the Topper was sandwiched between one's from Simple Minds - the day before - and The Pretenders the day after.

| GT gig | | 14 Jul | 79 |

Hunter
Rock band.

| GT gig | | 21 Aug | 77 |

The **Injectors**

Then Punk band. They laid down two tracks 'Frustration' and 'Welcome To Our Club,' which have recently surfaced on *Bored Teenagers Volume 3* punk compilation album.

| GT gig | | 14 Jun | 79 |
| | | 19 Aug | 79 |

After Became Mod revival band The Circles, signed a record deal, released several singles before splitting in 1981. They reformed in 1999 and a year later released the album *Looking Back* which was well received.

| The **Invaders** | 17 Jun | 79 |

| **Isotone** | 28 Jun | 75 |

The **Ivy League**
60's vocal/harmony band.

| GT gig | | 6 Jan | 74 |
| | | 27 Apr | 75 |

Record	Funny How Love Can Be	4 Feb	65	8
	That's Why I'm Crying	6 May	65	22
	Tossing and Turning	24 Jun	65	3

| **Jackdaw** | 11 Jul | 76 |

| **Jade Lemon** | 2 May | 69 |

Jaffa Band   20 Feb 71

The **Jags**

Then   New Wave, power pop band from Yorkshire. With a sound similar in vein to Elvis Costello and Nick Lowe. Band line-up – Nick Watkinson (vocals), John Alder (guitar/ backing vocals), Steve Prudence (bass), Alex Baird (drums).

GT gig   24 Jun 79

Record   Back Of My Hand   8 Sep 79   17

After/now   Released a couple of albums *Evening Standard* and *No Tie Like The Present* before splitting in 1982. Nick Watkinson has worked on various projects including *The White Fence* album with ex-Squeeze bass player Keith Wilkinson. John Alder is a successful composer, session musician, filmmaker and video artist. Alex Baird is a drum teacher. Steve Prudence whereabouts unknown.

Jimmy **James**
British soul singer.

GT Gig   7 Apr 74

Record   Red Red Wine   11 Sep 68   8
            I'll Go Where The Music -
            - Takes Me   26 Apr 76   8
            Now Is The Time   17 Jul 76   9

Jasper   8 Mar 75

The **Jerks**
Punk band formed by five teenagers from Yorkshire after witnessing the 'Anarchy In The UK' tour in 1976. Their single 'Get Your Woofing Dog Off Me' charted in 1978. Other tracks were 'Dole Queue Boys,' 'You're Not Worth It (Jerk Off)' and 'I'm So Bored With My School.' A compilation of live performances *We Hate You* was released in 1999.

GT gig   15 Apr 79
                                        12 May 79

Jigsaw

Very 70's soft pop band fronted by duo Clive Scott and Des Dyer. Had two Top 40 hits with 'Sky High' (9) and 'If I Have To Go Away' (36). They did go away but unfortunately the song writing pair are still in the music business and are responsible (very irresponsible more like) for songs by Bad Boys Inc and Boyzone.

GT gig		29 May 77

Jody	13 Aug 74

Judas Priest

Then	Young heavy rock group from the West Midlands.		
GT gig		20 May 75	
		12 Aug 75	
		21 Oct 75	
Record	Rocka Rolla (album)	74	-
	Sad Wings Of Destiny	76	-

After   Multi-million selling, leather clad and studded metal superstars. Laid the foundations and were hugely influential on speed and death metal.

In the late 1980's Judas Priest were taken to court in America after they were blamed for the attempted suicides of two youths. It was alleged that James Vance and Ray Belknap shot themselves after repeatedly listening to the Judas Priest album *Stained Class* which, it was claimed, contained evil subliminal messages. Vance died, Belknap survived but suffered severe facial disfigurement. No proof of this was found and the $6 million lawsuit was rejected.

Record	Take On The world	20 Jan 79	14
	Living After Midnight	29 Mar 80	12
	Breaking The Law	7 Jun 80	12

Now   Lead singer Robert Halford left the band to pursue solo projects, but now the original line-up - and the one that played the Grey Topper in 1975 - are back together.

Kenny

Then   Manufactured teen glam rock band. Debut single 'The Bump' (originally a Bay City Rollers b-side) was actually a product of producers and session musicians. When it reached the Top 40 and *Top Of The Pops* called, a real group was needed to appear as Kenny. A young band called Chuff, who's sound and appearance fitted the bill, were hastily recruited.

One of the session musicians used for their hits was Chris Spedding, who had a hit with 'Motor Biking,' but is best known for his work with the Sex Pistols on their early demos.

GT gig		23 Feb 75	
Record	The Bump	7 Dec 74	3
	Fancy Pants	8 Mar 75	4
	Baby I Love you Ok	7 Jun 75	12
	Julie Ann	16 Aug 75	10

After   The project came to an end after one of the band was seriously injured in a car crash. Children's TV presenter Timmy 'Mallet's' Mallet did a cover of 'The Bump' in 1991.

Ben E King

R&B singer - born Benjamin Earl Nelson 28/9/38. Became lead singer in soul group The Drifters in the early 1960's before having a successful solo career under the stage name Ben E King, most notably with the enduring classic 'Stand By Me' which – after being the theme tune to the film of the same name and featuring in a Levis ad – reached No.1 in 1987.

GT gig   25 Sep 76

After/now   Still touring and raising funds for his 'Stand By Me' charity organisation.

Kipper   30 Aug 76

Krazy Kat   2 Sep 75

L

The **Ladybirds**		18 Jul	76	
Benny Hill's backing singers.				

The **Lee Grant Explosion**		4 Nov	76	

Let The Good Times Roll		7 Jan	78	

Light Fantastic		MT		

Limelight		13 Oct	74	

Limmie and the Family Cookin
US soul group.

GT gig		31 Mar	74		
Record	You Can Do Magic	21 Jul	73		3
	Dreamboat	20 Oct	73		31
	A Walkin' Miracle	6 Apr	74		6

Little Acre		11 Apr	76	

Little Bo Bitch
New Wave band. Released a couple of singles in 1979 'It's Only Love,' 'Take It Easy' (both failed to chart), and the album *Little Bo Bitch*. Changed their name to the Lonely Boys as American radio stations were offended by the word 'Bitch' apparently.

GT gig		30 Jun	79	

Liverpool Express

Then	Saccharine 70's pop band formed by Billy Kinsley, formerly of The Merseybeats. Toured with Rod Stewart.				
GT gig		22 Feb	76		
Record	You Are My Love	26 Jun	76		11
	Everyman Must Have -				
	- A Dream	18 Dec	76		17

Love Lines	14 Oct 76
Love Machine	28 Jan 77

Magic Lanterns

Manchester based psychedelic band. Formed by Jimmy Bilsbury (vocals). Kevin Godley and Lol Crème were in the band at one time as was Ozzy Osbourne. No stop! Despite rumours to the contrary this is not THE Ozzy Osbourne, this was bass player Mike Osbourne. Many an unscrupulous record dealer has sold Magic Lanterns albums for astronomical fees with pretence of it being a rare release by the future Black Sabbath and US TV superstar.

Magic Lanterns did for a time have well-known singer/songwriter THE Albert Hammond in their ranks father of THE Albert Hammond Jr of The Strokes fame.

They had a Top 30 hit in the American billboard charts with 'Shame Shame' in 1969 from the album of the same name.

GT gig		27 Sep 69
		30 Nov 69
Record	Excuse Me Baby	7 Jul 66
	Shame Shame (album)	69

Mandarin Kraze   MT

Marmalade

First Scottish pop group to top the British charts with their version of The Beatles 'Ob-La-Di Ob-La-Da' in 1968. Achieved 8 Top 10 hits in all between 1968-76. Others were debut single 'Lovin' Things,' 'Reflections Of My Life' and 'Rainbow.'

GT gig   MT

Matchbox
One of Britain's most successful Rockabilly bands, that had a string of hits worldwide after their breakthrough single 'Rockabilly Rebel' (18) in 1979.

GT gig   28 Jan   78

Maxim   MT

Maxwell's Silver Hammer 15 Aug 74

Medicine Head
Innovative rock and blues duo - John Fiddler (vocals, guitar, piano, drums) and Peter Hope-Evans (harmonica, jew's harp, mouthbow), came to the attention of Radio 1's John Peel who booked them for a session, signed them to his Dandelion record label and produced (with his wife 'Pig' and friends) their debut album *New Bottles, Old Medicine*.
Chart success followed with the singles '(And The) Pictures In The Sky' (22), 'One And One Is One' (3), 'Rising Sun' (11) and 'Slip and Slide' (22). Played one of their last gigs at the Grey Topper.

GT gig   22 Jan   77
                                          23 Apr   77

Megella And The Derry Aires
Irish music band.   7 Apr 79

The **Members**
New Wave, punk band with elements of reggae in their sound. Singer/songwriter Nick Tesco's satirical lyrics and the band's punk credentials came to the fore on the classic era defining single 'Sound Of The Suburbs,' that had just lit up the charts when they came to the Grey Topper.
Their line up was Nick Tesco (vocals), JC Carroll (guitar/vocals), Nigel Bennett (guitar), Chris Payne (bass), Adrian Lillywhite (drums).

It was Adrian's brother Steve Lillywhite – who produced their brilliant debut album *At The Chelsea Nightclub*.

GT gig		22 Apr 79	
		22 Sep 79	
Record	Sound Of The Suburbs	3 Feb 79	12
	Offshore Banking Business	7 Apr 79	31

After   After three more albums the band split in 1983 on returning from a tour of America. Nick Tesco and JC Carroll are still involved with the music industry and in 2006 The Members performed for the first time in 24 years at JC's birthday bash.

Merlin   4 Dec 76

Merton Parkas

Then   Mod revivalist band from the south London area of Merton. The band line up was Danny Talbot (vocals), brother Mick (keyboards), Neil Wurrell (bass) and Simon Smith (drums).

GT gig		7 Oct 79	
Record	You Need Wheels	4 Aug 79	40

After/now   Mick Talbot briefly joined Dexy's Midnight Runners before teaming up with The Jam's Paul 'the modfather' Weller to form The Style Council, who had several Top 10 hits such as 'My Ever Changing Moods.' Also worked with Weller on his solo albums.

The **Merseybeats**
Part of the Liverpool beat sound of the 60's. Played alongside The Beatles at the famous Cavern Club and were originally signed by the fab four's manager Brian Epstein.

GT gig		MT	
Record	I Think Of you	16 Jan 64	5
	Don't Turn Around	16 Apr 64	13
	Wishin' And Hopin'	9 Jul 64	13

Method	6 Apr 78
McArthur Park	MT
Mickey's Monkey's	4 Dec 75

The Mighty Avons
Irish folk/country band   14 Apr 79

Miranda	6 Aug 76

Mojos
60's Merseybeat group who had three Top 40 hits with 'Everything's Alright' (9), 'Why Not Tonight' (25) and 'Seven Daffodils' (30). At one time actor Lewis Collins (*The Professionals*, *Who Dares Wins*) was part of the band.

GT gig   12 Feb 77

Montana's	MT
Monty	10 Sep 74
The **Moon Pennies**	6 Sep 69

Moonrider
Short lived rock group that had in their ranks - Elvis Costello and the Attraction's (and former Bitter Suite) bassist Bruce Thomas, John Weider (formerly of The Animals) and Keith West (who reached No.2 in the singles chart in 1967 with 'Excerpt From A Teenage Opera' and was also vocalist with innovative psychedelic group Tomorrow who supported and jammed with Jimi Hendrix).

GT gig   27 May 75
Mother Superior   9 Sep 75

Motor Biking
Jacksdale is as well-known for its motorbike connections as it is for its rock credentials. Two top racers have lived in

the village - John Newbold and Steve Henshaw. Newbold was Barry Sheene's Suzuki teammate in the 70's. Those two, along with 'Rocket' Ron Haslam, once appeared at a charity fund raising night at the Topper.

After   John Newbold was killed in a road race in Ireland in 1982. 'We brought his body back on the ferry. On there was the bike he'd died on, they wanted it back for parts or to rebuild it. There was no way that was going to happen, so we tipped it over the side into the sea,' Ally Key (who's daughter Alison was married to John Newbold).

Former World Champion Barry Sheene died of cancer aged 52 in 2003.

After 30 successful years racing Ron Haslam now coaches his son Leon who is making his name as a Superbike rider. Steve Henshaw also died in a road race.

Now   2010 – Jacksdale motorbike whiz kid - 13-year-old Kyle Ryde - becomes the youngest ever rider to appear at a British Superbike Championship meeting, sets lap records at Silverstone and Darleymoor and is selected for the Red Bull Rookies 'star finder' series.

Moving Finger   4 Jan   74

Mud

Then   After making their TV debut on the *Basil Brush Show*, this Rock 'n' roll influenced band became chart toppers of the mid 1970's. 'Tiger Feet' went No.1 in Jan 74 and was the biggest selling single of that year and was just one of ten Top 10 hits, which included Christmas No.1 'Lonely This Christmas.' The band line up consisted of Les Gray (vocals), Rob Davis (guitar), Dave Mount (drummer), Ray Stiles (bass).

GT gig   20 Jun   70
                                     17 Jan   71
                                     18 Feb   71

After/now Les Gray split from Mud in 1978, and released a solo single 'A Groovy Kind of Love,' but this barely dented the Top 40.

Soon he was back on the touring circuit with 'Les Gray's Mud.' In 2003 he was diagnosed with throat cancer, but he refused an operation to remove his voice box, so he could continue to sing, choosing chemotherapy as an alternative treatment. He died of a heart attack at his home in Portugal in 2004, aged 57.

Rob Davis has become a successful pop songwriter, hits include Kylie Minogue's 'Can't Get You Out Of My Head.' Ray Stiles toured with the Hollies.

Dave Mount is no longer in the music business.

Muffin   18 May 74

Mungo Jerry

Then   1970's London chart toppers, fronted by the unmistakable perm topped, huge sideburns and gap toothed smiling Ray Dorset. Released one of the best ever feel good hits of the summer 'In The Summer Time,' that went to No.1 in 1970 and stayed there for 7 weeks. Many hits followed.

GT gig   9 Jun   74

Record   In The Summertime   6 Jun   70   1
            Baby Jump   20 Feb   71   1
            Lady Rose   29 May 71   5
            Alright Alright Alright 7 Jul   73   3

After/now   Mungo Jerry have remained popular and still perform today. Ray Dorset has been a successful performer and songwriter in his own right, penning many songs including Kelly Marie's disco No.1 'Feels Like I'm In Love.'

Muscles   2 Nov 75

Mustard   20 Aug 74

Nashville Teens
1960's pop group, not from Nashville, but from Weybridge, Surrey.

GT gig		15 Jun	75	
Record	Tobacco Road	9 Jul	64	6
	Google Eye	22 Oct	64	10

Natural High 25 Jan 79

Don't know if this was a band or a chilled out social gathering at the Topper!

The **Nelson Family** 31 Jul 76

New Federation 21 Feb 71

New Formula 1 May 69

Nicol and Marsh

Acoustic/rock duo Ken Nicol (later with The Albion Band) and Pete Marsh (later to release a single with Vangelis)

GT gig 5 Aug 75

Nosmo King

Northern Soul. Charted in 1974 with The Javells with 'Goodbye Nothing To Say' (26).

GT gig 19 Mar 71

Nutz

Heavy metal band who toured with Black Sabbath and produced four albums – *Nutz, Nutz Too, Hard Nutz*, and erm *Nutz Live Cutz*.

In 2010 a new album *Nutz Live In Nottingham* was released, which was actually recorded by Radio Trent at the Grey Topper, Jacksdale (guess they thought that didn't look as cool on the sleeve?)

GT gig	10 Jun	75
	7 Oct	75

■

Ocean   2 May 74

Octopus

Then   Formerly The Cortinas ('Phoebe's Flower Shop') they became psychedelic band Octopus in 1967. Released one album *Restless Night* in 1969.

The band line up was Paul Griggs (vocals/guitar), brother Nigel Griggs (bass), Malcolm Green (drums), John Cook (keyboards).

GT gig   17 Jul   69

                                     8 Jan   70

After   Octopus split in 1972. Malcolm Green and Nigel Griggs later joined New Zealand New Wave band Split Enz (around the same time as Neil Finn later of Crowded House). John Cook worked with Mungo Jerry.

O'Hara's Playboys   MT

The **Ones That Got Away**

Tina Turner – money that's what she wanted, too much. The Sex Pistols – negotiations were taking place to bring them to the Topper before they imploded. The Cure – the Grey Topper is on the 'Boys Don't Cry' tour poster and many of their fan web sites list them as having played Jacksdale in 1979, but I don't believe they did in the end. The Skids – some say they played, others disagree. They're not pencilled into an exact date on the Grey Topper booking list for 1979 but are written in the margin. Sally Renshaw – a young punk at the time – saw some of the bands rehearse inside the Topper and thinks one of these were The Skids as some lads got the band to change the lyrics of 'Into The Valley' to 'Into The Sally' to sing to her for a laugh. The debate goes on.

Orange Bicycle

Then   Psychedelic band. Formed by keyboardist and songwriter Wilson Malone. Had a No.1 in France with the single

221

'Hyacinth Threads.' This also caught the attention of John Peel who played it on his *Perfumed Garden* show and went on to produce their album.

GT gig   24 Apr 69

After   The band split in 1971. After several other projects Will Malone became a producer and did the string arrangements on The Verve's 'Bittersweet Symphony' (one of my favourite ever records so good man).

Our Way Of Life   15 Nov 74

The **Overlanders**
UK folk trio who reached No.1 in 1966 with a version of The Beatles 'Michelle.'

GT gig   23 Nov 75

Owl   15 Jan 76

Paper Lace
Local band that hit the big time after winning TV talent show *Opportunity Knocks*. Topped the charts on both sides of the Atlantic.

GT gig   19 Feb 70
                                          22 Oct 76

Record   Billy Don't Be A Hero   23 Feb 74   1
          The Night Chicago Died   4 May 74   3
          The Black Eyed Boys   24 Aug 74   11

Parachute   MT

Paradox   3 Aug 78

Patchwork   7 Apr 77

Penny Whistle   9 Jul 76

Pepper Tree	1 Mar 75

Pepper Village	21 Nov 74

The **Pigboy Charlie Band**

Then   Rock and blues band from Canvey Island. Formed by Lee Brilleaux (vocals) and Chris Fenwick (jugs, then manager) and John Sparkes.

GT gig	30 Jan 71

After   The Pigboy's recruited Wilko Johnson on guitar and evolved into pub rock favourites Dr Feelgood, best known for their Top 10 single 'Milk and Alcohol' (9).
Wilko Johnson left Dr Feelgood to join Ian Dury's Blockheads, then formed his own band The Wilko Johnson Band (that still tour).
Lee Brilleaux stayed front man of Dr Feelgood until dying of cancer in 1994 aged 41.

Now   Julien Temple - director of the Sex Pistols films *The Great Rock 'n' Roll Swindle* and *The Filth And The Fury* - made an award winning film about Dr Feelgood called *Oil City Confidential* (that mentions the Topper gig). This has sent the popularity of the reformed band souring again.

Pinpoint

Then   Punk/New Wave band formed by Arturo Bassick after leaving The Lurkers ('The English Ramones'). Pinpoint supported The Members at the Topper. Around the time they released their debut single 'Richmond.'

GT gig	22 Apr 79

After   Arturo Bassick has worked with The Lurkers again and 999.

Pipers Moon	10 Sep 77

The **Pirates**

The Pirates started out as the backing band for rock 'n' roll singer Johnny Kid in the 1960's and had several hit singles including 'Shakin' All Over' (1) and 'I'll Never Get Over You' (4). In 1966 The Pirates split from Kidd (who shortly afterwards died in a car crash) to become a powerful R&B band.

GT gig   28 Apr 79

Richie **Pitts**
Northern Soul singer formerly of The Velours and The Fantastics

GT gig   4 May 74

Ponders End
John Parr, from the Nottingham mining town Worksop, put his first band The Silence together at the age of 12. When that project folded he formed Ponders End and toured the Northern clubs but failed to get a record deal.

GT gig   2 Jul   78

After   John Parr signed a publishing deal with Carlin Music and his song writing abilities were recognised by Meat Loaf, who asked him to work with them on their new album.
The Who's manager John Wolfe spotted his musical abilities and secured a record deal for Parr in America. Soon he was a successful solo artist, topping the US charts with the theme tune to 'brat pack' film *St Elmo's Fire*. The song and video for this are American 80's pop incarnate.

Record   St Elmo's Fire   2 Sep   85   6

Now   A successful singer, songwriter and composer on many films, John Parr is also now screenwriter and film producer.

Jimmy **Powell**
R&B singer from Birmingham. His backing group in the 1960's, The Five Dimensions, included a young Rod Stewart on harmonica and vocals. Also recorded a single with Jimmy Page and John Paul Jones later of Led Zeppelin fame.

GT gig		17 Aug 74

Pressure   12 Dec 74

The **Pretenders**

Then
American Chrissie Hynde settled in England, had a stint as an *NME* journalist, a shop assistant in 'Seditionaries' and after hanging around with the Sex Pistols formed her own band The Pretenders in 1978, recruiting Hertfordshire trio – Peter Farndon (bass), James Honeyman-Scott (guitar) and Martin Chambers (drums).

Record	Stop Your Sobbing	10 Feb 79	34
GT gig		18 Mar 79	
Record	Kid	14 Jul 79	33
GT gig		15 Jul 79	

After
Four months after playing their 2nd and last gig at the Topper their single 'Brass In Pocket' went to No.1 in the UK charts and broke them in America. The critically acclaimed album *Pretenders* was released in January 1980.

A few years later the original band were torn apart by the drug related deaths of Peter Farndon (heroin overdose) and James Honeyman-Scott (heart failure from cocaine intolerance).

Chrissie Hynde reformed the band and continued to have chart success including several more No.1's. The Pretenders are still hugely popular today.

Purple Shadow   6 May 76

Quartz
NWOBHM (New Wave Of British Heavy Metal) band – that started out as Bandylegs – from Birmingham. Gained the attention of Black Sabbath's Tony Iommi who produced their debut album *Quartz*, this had an uncredited

Ozzy Osbourne on backing vocals and Queen's Brian May also played on some tracks.

Line up – Mike Taylor (vocals) Geoff Nichols (guitar, keyboard. Later joined Black Sabbath), Mike Hopkins (guitar), Derek Arnold (bass), Malcolm Cope (drums).

GT gig   6 May 79
                                          8 Jul   79

Quill
Folk band   MT

Race Against Time
NWOBHM band   26 Aug 79

Racing Cars
Welsh soft-rock band. Did several sessions for John Peel and tasted chart success when their single 'They Shoot Horses Don't They' which reached No.7 in 1977.

GT gig   4 Feb   79

Rain   MT

Rainbow Cottage
Pop band.

GT gig   28 Aug 70

Record   Seagull   6 Mar   76   33

Rainbow Valley   MT

Razzle   MT

Rebel Rousers
Formerly - with Cliff Bennett - they were signed by Brian Epstein and toured with The Beatles who gave them the song 'Got To Get You Into My Life' (written for the 'Revolver' album) to record, it reached No.6 in the Charts.

After splitting with Cliff Bennett, the Rebel Rousers released the mod single 'Should I.'

GT gig		10 Apr 69
Redhead		15 Apr 74
Rio		25 Nov 76

Ritz
NWOBHM band. Released one single 'Love Till The Day I Die'/ 'Keep Dancing.' Changed their name to Berlin Ritz in 1980. Continue to do gigs and record but never really rose above the level they were at in 1979.

GT gig		27 Aug 79
		23 Dec 79

Rokotto
UK Disco/funk band

GT gig		16 Apr 78	
Record	Boogie On Up	22 Oct 77	40
	Funk Theory	10 Jun 78	49

Roy Hill Band
Singer/songwriter that had a record deal, did two sessions for John Peel but never fulfilled his promise. He is, however, still very popular on the club circuit, well known for his comic monologues between songs. Played at the tribute show for the late, great John Peel.

GT gig		11 Feb 79

Rubettes

Then   Doo-wop, rock 'n' roll, influenced UK pop band in the mid 1970's. Usually decked out in white suits and caps. Their debut single 'Sugar Baby Love' sold eight million copies worldwide.

GT gig		12 Jan 75

Record	Sugar Baby Love	4 May 74	1
	Tonight	13 Jul 74	12
	Juke Box Jive	16 Nov 74	3
	I Can Do It	8 Mar 75	7

After   The Rubettes split in 1979. However following a huge surge in popularity for such music in Germany they got back together in 1983.
Guitarist Tony Thorpe - under the guise of Moody Boyz -later became a techno, acid, jungle, pioneering producer. Mixed tracks for KLF and released novelty track 'Star Trekkin' under the name The Firm.

Now   Following another acrimonious split and court case, more than one version of The Rubettes tour the nostalgia circuit.

Jimmy **Ruffin**

American Motown soul singer, best known for his Top 10 hit 'What Becomes of the Brokenhearted.'

GT gig   -   -   73

Rufus featuring **Chaka Khan**

Funk/soul band that had female lead singer Chaka Khan who, it was said, put so much into her vocal delivery that 'she once vomited into the crowd,' (wonder if this was the Topper, she could have had a pint of local brew?)

GT gig   72-75

Record   After splitting from Rufus, Chaka Khan became a hugely popular solo artist. Best known in the UK for her No.1 hit 'I Feel For You' in 1984.

The **Ruts**

Then   Staunchly anti-racist with powerful, reggae influenced, anthemic songs, The Ruts were one of the best of the second wave of punk bands.
Fronted by the charismatic singer Malcolm Owen, other band members were – Paul Fox (guitar), Vince Segs (bass), Dave Ruffy (drums). Championed by John Peel their single

'Babylon's Burning' smashed it's way into the Top 10 in the summer of 1979.

GT gig		16 Sep 79	
Record	Babylon's Burning	16 Jun 79	7
	Something That I Said	8 Sep 79	29
	Staring At The Rude Boys	19 Apr 80	22

After   Malcolm Owen died of a drugs overdose on July 14th 1980. The rest of the band carried on for a while as Ruts D C but could never fill the gaping void left by Owen and split in 1983.

Now   Dave Ruffy is a successful session drummer (having worked with the likes of Aztec camera, Sinead O'Connor, Adam Ant and The Waterboys) Produced the World's first live drum loop CD and 'arguably the finest dance drum CD ever' with *Ruff Cuts*.

Segs is in the band Alabama 3, best known for 'Woke Up This Morning' the theme tune to the TV series *The Sopranos*.

For the first time in over 20 years Paul Fox had started playing The Ruts music again in 2006 with his new band Foxy's Ruts. Several months later he was diagnosed with cancer and died in October 2007 aged 56.

Salt
Hard rock and blues band. Only recorded one 4 track EP 'All Wired Up,' but played the Reading Festival and once co-headlined with the Sex Pistols at the 100 club.

GT gig   10 May 77

Salty Dog   12 Jan 78

Sam Apple Pie
UK blues/rock band. They appeared at the first ever Glastonbury Festival (1970 attended by about 2000 people) along with T Rex. Jammed with Frank Zapper.

Sassafras

Welsh progressive rock band. Appeared on the BBC2 music show *The Old Grey Whistle Test*, best known for their *Wheelin' and Dealin'* album.

GT gig   MT

Saxon

Started out as Son Of A Bitch before changing their name to Saxon in 1977 and becoming pioneers of the New Wave Of British Heavy Metal movement. Had just released their debut album *Saxon*, from which the single 'Big Teaser/ Stallions Of The Highway' was taken and was riding high in the heavy metal charts but failing to dent the Top 100.

GT gig   12 Aug 79

After/now   Saxon became one of the biggest heavy metal bands of the 1980's after the release of their second album *Wheels Of Steel*, the single of the same name reached No.20 and the follow up *747 (Strangers In The Night)* peaked at No.13. They continue to have a huge following, record and tour.
Trivia; It is rumoured that the classic mockumentary film *This Is Spinal Tap* was based on Saxon.

Screaming Lord Sutch

Eccentric horror-themed rock musician. Best known for upstaging MP's at elections by standing against them with his 'Monster Raving Loony Party.' As a singer he released the single 'Jack The Ripper' (produced by the legendary Joe Meek). Upon its release it was banned by the BBC. A cult classic, it has since been covered by the White Stripes, The Horrors, The Fall and Black Lips.

GT gig   MT

Shakin' Stevens And The Sunsets

Then   Rock 'n' roll band that shared the bill with the Rolling Stones and David Bowie, was voted the 'best live act' of

1972 by *NME*, had a huge following in Holland, but failed to break into the UK charts.

| GT gig | 19 Dec 70 |

After   After splitting from his band in 1977, Shakin' Stevens became the top selling UK singles artist of the 80's with hits like 'This Ole House' (1) and 'Green Door' (1).
Trivia; famously attacked Richard Madeley (*Richard and Judy*) on a TV pop show in the 80's.

Del **Shannon**

Rock 'n' roll singer best known for the No.1 hit 'Runaway' on which an early form on synthesizer – a musitron – was used. Fatally shot himself with a .22 calibre rifle in 1990.

| GT gig | 6 Apr 74 |

| **Sidewinder** | 29 Jan 76 |

| The **Silhouettes** | 2 Feb 71 |

| **Silver Cloud** | 30 Nov 74 |

Simple Minds

Then   New Wave band formed in Glasgow by school friends Jim Kerr and Charlie Burchill after their punk band Johnny And The Self Abusers split in 1978. Simple Minds were signed to Zoom Records and had released their debut album and single both called *Life In A Day* in the spring of 1979. Second single was 'Chelsea Girl' but failed to chart.

GT gig	13 Jul 79	
Record	Life In A Day	12 May 79	62
	Chelsea Girl	1 Jun 79	-

After/now   In 1982 their critically acclaimed album *New Gold Dream* catapults them to pop fame. Five of their albums would enter the charts at No.1 and sell 30 million worldwide. In 1985 the single 'Don't You (Forget About Me)' breaks them in America after it is featured in the cult teen film *The*

Breakfast Club. The same year they play Live Aid (Philadelphia) in front of 90,000 people on the same date they'd played the Grey Topper in 1979.

Simple Minds are still together.

Record	Promised You A Miracle	10 Apr 82	13
	Don't You (Forget - - About Me)	20 Apr 85	7
	Alive And Kicking	12 Oct 85	7
	Belfast Child	18 Feb 89	1

Sinceros

Then   New Wave band formed by Mark Moesgaard Kjelden (vocals/ guitar) and one-time Vibrator Don Snow (keyboards). Their rhythm section Ron Francois (bass) and Bobby Irwin (drums) helped their breakthrough by backing Lene Lovich on tour and in the studio. Signed to Columbia Records they released the album *The Sound Of Sunbathing* in 1979.

GT gig   7 Jul   79

After/now Don Snow (now Jonn Savannah) joined Squeeze, then was a solo artist, session musician (touring with Tina Turner, Van Morrison and Roger Daltry), had a group called The Catch who were huge in Germany, and in 2002 performed 10 different character voices for a French comedy film.

Ron Francois worked with Julian Cope's Teardrop Explodes and Bobby Irwin played drums for Van Morrison.

Sky   69 - 71

Smiffy   MT

Sore Throat

Short-lived New Wave/punk band. They released a couple of singles 'Zombie Rock/ I Don't Want To Go Home,' 'Kamikaze Kid' and the album *Sooner Than You Think*.

GT gig   5 May 79

| | | 30 Sep | 79 | |

| **Spasm** | | 25 Oct | 74 | |

| **Sparrow** | | 3 Nov | 74 | |

The **Specials**

Then

Hailing from Coventry The Specials fused punk and ska to create their own unique '2 Tone' sound. The label of the same name had just been formed by founder member Jerry Dammers and they were about to release their debut single 'Gangsters.' The band line up was Jerry Dammers (songwriter/ keyboards), Terry Hall (vocals), Lynval Golding (guitar/ vocals), Roddy Radiation (guitar), Neville Staples (percussion/ vocals), Sir Horace Gentleman (bass) and John Bradbury (drums).

| GT gig | | 23 Jun | 79 | |
| Record | Gangsters | 28 Jul | 79 | 6 |

After

Their legendary status was confirmed with the release of their debut album and a series of classic singles such as 'A Message To You Rudy' (10), a live EP featuring 'Too Much Too Young' (1), 'Rat Race' (5) and 'Ghost Town' (1) after which the original line up split.

Terry Hall, Neville Staples and Lynval Golding formed Fun Boy Three. Jerry Dammers Special A.K.A's Top 10 record 'Nelson Mandela' reached No.9 in the charts and helped bring awareness to the anti-apartheid cause and Mandela's continued imprisonment.

Now

The Specials - minus Jerry Dammers – reformed in 2009 to tour. They played many of the festivals including the Pyramid Stage at Glastonbury – I was there!

Staa Marx

New Wave band, released the single 'Crazy Weekend' in 1979.

| GT gig | | 2 Jun | 79 |

Alvin **Stardust**

Then Born Bernard William Jewry and brought up in the nearby mining town Mansfield. Changed his name to Shane Fenton when he became a pop singer in the 1950/60's. Changed his name again - when jumping on the glam rock bandwagon - to Alvin Stardust. With a disturbing look – glam crossed with Gene Vincent and his trademark black leather gloves – he had 7 Top 10 hits, the most famous being 'My Coo-Ca-Choo' (2). The follow up 'Jealous Mind' reached No.1

GT gig   71 - 73

After Now treads the theatre boards. Starred in musicals as Uriah Heap in *David Copperfield*, Billy Butlin in *The Butlins Story* and the Child Catcher in *Chitty Chitty Bang Bang*.

Edwin **Starr**

Then US Motown soul star. Most famous for his brilliant rendition of Vietnam War protest song 'War.'

GT gig   3 May 74

Record				
Stop Her On Sight	11 Dec	68	11
War	24 Oct	70	3
Stop The War Now	20 Feb	71	33

After Settled in England, he featured on many UK singles including No.1 single 'Let It Be' by Ferry Aid to raise money for the victims of the Zeebrugge ferry disaster, also collaborated with the Utah Saints. He died of a heart attack, aged 61, at his home in Nottingham in 2003 and is buried in the city's Southern cemetery.

Stormer   MT

Strange Days   MT

The **Stranglers**

Then After being on the road constantly (sometimes travelling in Jet Black's ice cream van) since forming as the 'Guilford Stranglers' in 1974 as part of the 'pub rock' scene, the group were just beginning to be associated with punk after touring with The Vibrators and having being booked to open for The Ramones.

No record deal at the time, but were just putting together a new demo tape that included 'Grip,' 'Bitching' and 'Go Buddy Go.'

Band members – Hugh Cornwell (vocals/guitar), Jean-Jacques Burnel (bass), Jet Black (drummer) and Dave Greenfield (keyboard).

GT gig	21 May 76

After   Signed by record label United Artist in December 1976 and became one of the most successful groups to emerge from the punk era with over twenty Top 40 hits including – 'Peaches' (8), 'Something Better Change' (9), 'No More Heroes' (8), 'Golden Brown' (2) and 'Strange Little Girl' (7)

Now   Hugh Cornwell left the band in 1990 and has had a successful career as a solo artist. The rest of the band recruited a new singer and have continued touring as The Stranglers.

Stray

Heavy rock group who produced several acclaimed albums such as *Suicide*, *Saturday Morning Pictures* and *Mudanzas* (that went gold). They supported Black Sabbath, Kiss and Rush and for a short time, in 1977, were managed by Charlie Kray, brother of the Kray Twins. Stray are still on the road today, not running from the Kray's though.

GT gig	26 Apr 77

Strife

Liverpool based heavy metal band acclaimed for their live performances. Toured with Jethro Tull, Procul Harum and Ian Gillan. In 2006 a live recording of one of their gigs at Nottingham Boat Club in 1976 was unearthed and released on CD to good reviews.

GT gig	22 Jul 75

22nd Street People 4 Jul 69

Sunrise 18 Aug 77

Supercharge
Rhythm and Blues rock band formed in Liverpool in 1974 by sax player and singer Albie Donelly. Opened for Queen in front of 100,000 people and had huge success in Australia where their album *Local Lads Made Good* went gold. Dropped by Virgin records during the punk era. A form of the band is still together.

GT gig 21 Jan 79

Superfly 4 Jan 76

Sweet
Glam rock superstars. The band consisted of Brian Connolly (lead vocals), Andy Scott (guitar), Steve Priest (bass), Mick Tucker (drums). Remembered as much for their androgynous glam image – glitter, platform sole boots, long hair and heavy make up (and famously Steve Priest's German military helmet and Nazi armband on *Top Of The Pops*) – as for their stomping pop anthems.

GT gig		7 Feb 71	
Record	Funny Funny	13 Mar 71	13
GT gig		28 Mar 71	
Record	Co-Co	12 Jun 71	2
GT gig		27 Aug 72	
Record	Wig-Wam-Bam	9 Sep 72	4
	Blockbuster	13 Jan 73	1
GT gig		8 Apr 73	

After The hits continued to flow with the likes of 'Ballroom Blitz' (2) and 'Teenage Rampage' (2). By the late 70's and the arrival of punk they were looking a bit dated and it was all but over when Brian Connolly left the band.

Now	Brian Connolly died of liver failure and a heart attack attributed to his chronic alcoholism, aged 51, in 1997. Mick Tucker died of leukaemia in 2002 aged 54. Steve Priest is a solo artist. Andy Scott tours with his band AS Sweet.			

Sweet Sensation

Then	Manchester soul band that shot to fame after appearing on the talent show *New Faces*.			
GT gig		24 Feb	74	
		29 Jun	74	
Record	Sad Sweet Dreamer	14 Sep	74	1
	Purely By Coincidence	18 Jan	75	11
After	Sweet Sensation split in 1977. Lead vocalist Marcel King had a single, 'Reach For Love' (produced by New Order's Bernard Sumner) released by Factory Records in 1991, but died of a brain haemorrhage at the age of 38 in 1995. Tragically his son Zeus was shot dead – a victim of Manchester gang warfare – two years later.			

The **Swinging Blue Jeans**
Liverpool beat group, resident at the famous Cavern Club in the early 60's, they gave a guest spot to up and coming group The Beatles. The Blue Jeans are best known for their No.2 single 'Hippy Hippy Shake' that led them to appear on the very first *Top Of The Pops*. During filming they had a punch up with the Rolling Stones.

GT gig		8 Oct	76
	Symbols	12 Jan	74

Take 4	10 Jul	76
Technique	16 Sep	74
Terrapin	MT	

237

Thumper	20 Jul	74	

Together	1 Jun	75	

The **Tourists**

Then   Pop band formed by Sunderland pair Pete Coombes and Dave Stewart. The latter's lover – Scottish, peroxide blonde Annie Lennox was recruited as singer. Making up the rest of the band where Eddie Chin (bass), Jim Toomey (drums).

GT gig		16 Jun	79	
Record	Blind Among Flowers	9 Jun	79	52

After   The Tourists went on to have two Top 10 hits 'I Only Want To Be With You' (4) and 'So Good To Be Back Home' (8) that had been performed at the Grey Topper before splitting in 1980. Stewart and Lennox became synth pop duo Eurythmics and gained international fame and millions of record sales with singles like 'Sweet Dreams' (2), 'Who's That Girl' (3), 'There Must Be An Angel' (1) and the album *Touch* (1).

Now   Pete Coombes died in 1997. After the split of Eurythmics in the 1990's Lennox has become a successful solo artist winning an Oscar for her song 'Into The West' from the film *The Lord Of The Rings: The Return Of The King* and performing at Live 8. Stewart continues to write songs and make film soundtracks. Recently Stewart and Lennox have worked together again as the Eurythmics.

Toyah

Then   Birmingham punk, singer and actress Toyah Wilcox first came to prominence playing 'Mad' in the film *Jubilee* and 'Monkey' in *Quadrophenia*. Her band were starting to get favourable reviews in the music press - and a huge punk following - after the release of six track EP 'Sheep Farming In Barnet.'

GT gig	9 Sep	79

After	Toyah Wilcox became one of the first iconic figures of 80's pop as her band achieved a number of chart hits. Voted best female singer at the 1983 *British Rock and Pop Awards*.

Record	Four From Toyah EP -		
	- (featuring 'It's A Mystery') 14 Feb 81	4
	I Want To Be Free	14 May 81	8
	Thunder In The Mountains	3 Oct 81	4

Now Successful actress (with stage roles such as Calamity Jane and Cruella De Vil), TV and Radio presenter (everything from *Songs Of Praise* to *The Good Sex Guide* and a stint on *I'm A Celebrity Get Me Out Of Here*). Still tours with her band on the 80's nostalgia circuit.

Trapeze
UK hard rock band whose members are better known for work they did with other bands. Glen Hughes (vocals) joined Deep Purple in 1973 before rejoining Trapeze for a short time in 1976/77, Mel Galley (vocals/guitar) later joined Whitesnake, Dave Holland (drums) joined Judas Priest, Peter Goalby was a member of Uriah Heap.

GT gig 1 Feb 77
5 Mar 78

The **Tremeloes**
1960's pop group, signed up to Decca records in preference to The Beatles who had auditioned for the label on the same day. They didn't become chart toppers until 1967 though, when 'Here comes My Baby' peaked at No.4 in the charts and 'Silence Is Golden' reached No.1. Many hits followed.

GT gig 1 Apr 71
5 Jan 75

Tristan Shandy MT

Troy 24 Sep 74

True Expression   11 Jan   76

Truth   19 Dec   74

The **Tymes**
US soul group. Had four Top 40 hits – 'So Much In Love,'
'People,' 'You Little Trustmaker' and 'Ms Grace.'

GT gig   31 Mar 75

Record   Ms Grace   21 Dec 74   1

UFO

Then   Influential (on Metallica for one) UK hard rock band. The
           line up at the time of their Grey Topper gig was – Phil
           Mogg (vocals), Michael Schenker (guitar), Pete Way (bass),
           Andy Parker (drums) and Danny Peyronel (guitar/
           keyboards).
           Their breakthrough album *Phenomenon* (which contained
           'Doctor, Doctor' and 'Rock Bottom') had been released in
           1974 and they had just followed it up with *Force It*.

GT gig   26 Aug 75

After   Schenker left the band in 1979 to join the The Scorpions,
           then had a successful solo career before recently rejoining
           UFO.

UK Subs

Then   Punk band formed in late 1976. With the classic line up of
           Charlie Harper (vocals), Nicky Garratt (guitar), Paul Slack
           (bass) and Pete Davies (drums), they came to Jacksdale
           twice during their most successful period, on the
           'Stranglehold' and *Another Kind Of Blues* tours. A run of
           seven Top 40 singles would secure their legend,
           emblazoned on leather jackets across the World.

GT gig   22 Jul   79
                                        14 Oct   79

Record	Stranglehold	23 Jun 79	26
	Tomorrows Girls	8 Sep 79	28
	She's Not There	1 Dec 79	36
	Warhead	8 Mar 80	30

After/now   The infamous riot gig at The Black Horse, Riddings (2 miles from Jacksdale) happened in the 1980's. The UK Subs (with various line-ups but always lead by the enduring Charlie Harper) continue to record and are seemingly forever on the road from America to Australia and in May 2007 they played a 'Grey Topper Punks Reunited' gig.

2010 - Won BBC 6 Music's Punk Rock World Cup, knocking out The Clash and The Sex Pistols on route to the final. On the victory over the latter Charlie Harper said, 'Country Life Butter? That's not punk.'

Ultravox!

Then   Yes note the exclamation mark, it's not that I'm surprised they played the Grey Topper, it was on the end of their name in those days, spring 1977. It could have been put there by someone listening to their eponymous titled debut album – which had just been released when they came to Jacksdale - and expecting synth powered anthems like 'Vienna.'

This Ultravox! – who's line up was John Foxx (vocals), Billy Currie (synthesiser, violin), Steve Shears (guitar), Chris Cross (bass) and Warren Cann (drums) – were a Bowie, Roxy Music (Brian Eno produced the album with Steve Lillywhite) influenced and sounding band, with elements of punk. It's only on tracks like 'My Sex' that the synth comes to the fore and give an indication of the future sound to come.

GT gig		22 Mar 77	

Record	Dangerous Rhythm/My Sex	4 Feb 77	-
	Ultravox! (album)	25 Feb 77	-
	Young Savage	28 May 77	-

After   Two more albums followed much in the same vein, but with a more electronic sound emerging, before they were dropped by Island Records in 1978. John Foxx went solo and had a Top 40 hit with synth laden 'Underpass.'

Billy Currie joined Visage for a time and composed 'Fade To Grey' (8) and also worked with Gary Numan on his *Pleasure Principle* album before returning to Ultravox.

Midge Ure from the Rich Kids was recruited as singer and they became synth/New Romantic superstars with massive hits like 'Vienna' (2), 'All Stood Still' (8) and 'Dancing With Tears In My Eyes' (3)

Now   John Foxx still records experimental electronic music and tours. Billy Currie is still in the music business. Chris Cross now works as a psychotherapist and counsellor. Warren Cann lives in LA.

Upp
Experimental jazz-fusion rock band that featured Yardbirds guitar legend Jeff Beck.

GT gig   16 Sep 75

The **Vagabonds**
Jamaican/UK soul band lead by Jimmy James. The original band in the 60's had a Top 40 hit with 'Red Red Wine,' and opened for The Who. After they disbanded Jimmy James put together a new group that became favourites on the UK Northern Soul circuit.

GT gig   13 Nov 77

Record	I'll Go Where Your Music -		
	- Takes Me	24 Apr 76	36
	Now Is The Time	17 Jul 76	5

Bobby **Vee**
US pop star of the early 1960's. Still tours today.

GT gig   12 May 74

Record	Rubber Ball	19 Jan 61	4
	More Than I Can Say	13 Apr 61	4
	Take Good Care Of -		
	- My Baby	26 Oct 61	3
	Run To Him	21 Dec 61	6
	The Night Has A -		
	- Thousand Eyes	7 Feb 63	3

The **Vibrators**

One of the original punk groups – formed February 1976 - their early gigs were supporting The Stranglers and Sex Pistols. Played at the legendary Punk Rock Festival at the 100 Club in 1976, which also had on the bill The Clash, Sex Pistols, Siouxsie and the Banshees, The Dammed and Buzzcocks.

When the The Vibrators came to Jacksdale they had just supported ex The Stooges Iggy Pop (with David Bowie on keyboards).

GT gig		3 May 77	
Record	We Vibrate	Nov 76	-
	Baby Baby	May 77	-
	Pure Mania (album)	May 77	49
	Automatic Lover	18 Mar 78	35
After	Knoxie and Eddy continue to tour and record music as The Vibrators.		
	John Ellis joined The Stranglers in the 1990's.		

Voyage
Euro disco group.

GT gig		14 Aug 76	
Record	From East To West	17 Jun 78	13

Wally   17 May 75
Where's Wally?

Geno Washington

Then   American soul singer. Settled in Britain after being based here whilst serving in the US air force. Then found fame with R&B The Ram Jam Band. Their two debut (live) LP's *Hand Clappin' Foot Stompin' Funky-Butt...Live!* and *Hipsters, Flipsters, Finger-Poppin' Daddies!* were huge Top 10 sellers. Supported by Cream, Jimi Hendrix and Pink Floyd.

GT gig   24 May 70

After   Dropped out of the music scene for a while studying hypnotism and meditation, until Dexy's Midnight Runners tribute single 'Geno' went to No.1 in 1981. With a resurgence in his popularity he began to tour and record again and has done so ever since.

Trivia; At a party in Manchester in 1984 he told a young Ian Brown 'you're a star, be a singer.' He took his advice and joined The Stone Roses.

Wheels   7 Jun 75

Whispering Wind   19 Feb 77

Why Not   4 Jul 76

Wicked Lady   9 Nov 75

Marty Wilde

Along with Cliff Richard and Tommy Steel, Wilde was one of the first British rock 'n' roll teen idols in the late 1950's and early 60's. Also father of 80's pop star Kim Wilde who he produced and wrote songs for.

GT gig   11 Dec 76

Xit   11 Oct 74

The **Yachts**

Then New Wave band from Liverpool. They started life as Albert And The Cod Fish Warriors supporting the Sex Pistols at a gig in 1976. As the Yachts they made their debut at famous Liverpool venue Eric's supporting Elvis Costello. Did a couple of John Peel sessions, the second of these in June 79 included the single 'Love you Love You.' An album followed on Radar Records.

GT gig   1 Jul   79

After The Yachts split in the early 80's. Keyboard player Henry Priestman found fame in the bands It's Immaterial, Wah! and The Christians. Bass player Martin Dempsey joined Pink Military and also It's Immaterial.

Zender Jacks
Blonde, bubble perm haired, female glam rock singer, managed by Peter Stringfellow. Had a single called 'Rub My Tummy.'

GT gig   11 May 75

Zenith   MT

Zipper   22 Aug 74

Zorro
Heavy metal band on tour to promote their 'Arrods Don't Sell Em' EP when they played the Topper. Split in 1980.
Zorro once knocked on the door of John Peel's home after playing a gig in Ipswich and were invited in for tea.
Drummer Ricci Titcombe joined novelty punk band Splodgenessabounds of 'Two Pints Of Lager And A Packet Of Crisps' fame.

GT gig   29 Nov 79

Acknowledgements

I started on the Grey Topper project in 2006, after seeing the old building being demolished, and after hearing the stories from the original Topper punks (they'd all become good friends of mine over the years.) The Grey Topper Punks Reunited concert in 2007 happened a month after my dad had died of cancer, so I was burnt out and put the project to one side for a while. My passion for it was re-ignited in 2009 after watching Sex Pistols film maker Julien Temple's latest music film *Oil City Confidential* on BBC4. It tells the story of pub rockers Dr Feelgood and – as featured in the book – mentions the Grey Topper. Writing the story (and building the website and putting on the concert) was always a labour of love and great fun though.

I never thought I'd be interviewing, making contact with and putting on a concert with childhood pop heroes of mine. Special mention has to go to – The Members, Nick Tesco and JC Carroll - The Specials, Roddy Byers - The Stranglers, Jet Black - Eddie from The Vibrators - Steve Hovington of B-Movie - Dr Feelgood manager Chris Fenwick - Alan Wilder (for putting down his memories for me on the road in the middle of Argentina) – Andy Scott and Steve Priest of The Sweet – Mensi of Angelic Upstarts – Phil Gilbert, The Jerks – Kelly Johnson, Girlschool, and last but not least UK Subs - Charlie Harper for coming to play the Grey Topper Punks Reunited concert in the middle of a world tour. Thanks to all those who gave their time.

Many thanks to the Topper crowd too of course, especially – Nige Spike Cockayne, Jeff Fenn, Mic Clark, Tink, Marsy, Malc Fletcher and Ally Key.

Thanks to Jet Black of The Stranglers for sending me the picture of his ice cream tour van for use in the book, this was taken by Garry Coward-Williams. And to Roddy Radiation for the use of his early Specials photograph – Ralph Amott for the picture of inside the Grey Topper 1973 – and everyone else who's pictures are used in the book.

I would also like to mention the following for their support – Owen Carne at www.stranglers.net for putting me in touch with Jet Black and providing info about The Stranglers 1976 – Mick Twomey at www.nottstalgia.com - BADJER News for spreading the word in Jacksdale – Andy Smart and Simon Wilson at *Nottingham Evening Post* – Clive Whittingham at *Ripley & Heanor News* – Martin Weiss at *Selston & Underwood AD* newspaper - Bill Parr (R.I.P.) and son Eric – Gary Roe – Singo - Stephen Fletcher – Tony Oglesby – Phil Hodgkinson – Ashley Durose – Keith Dixon – Simon Pilgrim – Showaddywaddy's Malcolm Allured and Lee at MFN club at Eastwood – Jason and all his regulars at Foremans Punk Rock bar in Nottingham for their support of the Grey Topper Punks Reunited concert.

Lightning Source UK Ltd.
Milton Keynes UK

175400UK00001B/250/P